THE SACRED FLAME

Originally produced at the Playhouse Theatre, London, on 8th February, 1929, and revived at the St. Martin's Theatre, London, on 22nd November, 1945, with the following cast of characters :—

(in the order of their appearance)

MAURICE TABRET	*Ian Lubbock*
DR. HARVESTER	*Donald Strachan*
MRS. TABRET	*Mary Hinton*
NURSE WAYLAND	*Sonia Dresdel*
ALICE	*Pat Clarance*
MAJOR LICONDA	*Gordon McLeod*
STELLA TABRET	*Mary Martlew*
COLIN TABRET	*Ronald Millar*

The Play produced by GEOFFREY WARDWELL.

The action takes place at Gatley House,
Mrs. Tabret's residence, near London.

THE SACRED FLAME

ACT 1

SCENE.—The drawing-room at Gatley House.

It is a large easy room furnished comfortably in rather an old-fashioned way, with spacious chairs covered in faded chintz, great bowls of flowers, English china, Victorian water colours and photographs in silver frames. It is the drawing-room of an elderly lady who has furnished it in the way she has since her childhood known a drawing-room furnished. An interior decorator has never been inside the door. No stranger entering it would cry, " How lovely ! " but if he were sensitive to his surroundings he might think it a very good room to eat muffins in for tea and he would slip his hand behind the cushions on the settee in the certainty that he would find fat little lavender bags in the corners.
(See the Ground Plan and Furniture Plot.)

It is now the height of June, the weather is very fine, and the french windows that lead into the garden are wide open. Through them you see the starry radiant night.

When the CURTAIN *rises, it discovers* MAURICE *and* MRS. TABRET, NURSE WAYLAND, *and* DR. HARVESTER. MRS. TABRET *is seated on the settee, working at her tapestry. She is a slim, small, grey-haired lady, with a gentle manner, but her face is determined; it has a ravaged look as though fate had borne her many a blow, but also a serenity that suggests that she has found in herself the character and the courage to put up a good fight. She is dressed in semi-evening dress, in black.* NURSE WAYLAND, *seated in the easy chair below the settee, is reading a book. She is a girl of twenty-seven or so, handsome rather than pretty, with fine eyes, a little sullen, perhaps, and in her expression the hungry, somewhat pathetic look that some women have at her age. She is dressed not in uniform, but in a pretty, simple frock that sets off her fine figure.* DR. HARVESTER *and* MAURICE *are playing chess.* DR. HARVESTER *is the family doctor; he is a youngish man, fresh complexioned and of an open countenance, fair, clean and amiable. He wears a dinner jacket and is seated* L. *of the table* L.C. MAURICE *is lying on an invalid bed, in pyjamas and a bed-jacket. He is trim and neat, with his hair close-cropped and his face fresh-shaven; he has a handsome head and his manner is cheerful and even hearty; but he is very thin, his cheeks are pale and hollow, and his dark eyes look enormous. But they are constantly smiling. He gives no sign of being sorry for himself. There is a pause while the doctor considers the situation.*

MAURICE (*with good-humoured sarcasm*). Speed is the essence of this game, old boy !

HARVESTER. Don't let the brute bully me, Mrs. Tabret.

MRS. TABRET (*smiling*). I think you're quite capable of taking care of yourself, Doctor.

(*A pause while* HARVESTER *considers the game again.*)

MAURICE. If you moved your bishop you'd make things a bit awkward for me.

HARVESTER (*imperturbably, considering the game*). When I want your advice, I'll ask for it.

MAURICE. Mother, is that the way respectable general practitioners talked to their patients in the days of your far-distant youth ?

MRS. TABRET. How on earth do you expect poor Nurse Wayland to read when you never for an instant hold your tongue ? I can't even hear myself tatting.

NURSE (*looking up for an instant, with a pleasant smile*). I don't mind, Mrs. Tabret, don't bother about me.

MAURICE. After listening to my sprightly conversation for nearly five years Nurse Wayland pays no more attention to me than if I were a deaf mute.

MRS. TABRET (*dryly*). Who can blame her ?

MAURICE (*cheerily*). Even when pain and anguish wring my brow and I swear like fifty thousand troopers I never manage to bring the blush of shame to her maiden cheek.

NURSE (*smiling*). I know it's exasperating.

MAURICE (*looking across at* NURSE WAYLAND). It's worse than that, Nurse. It's inconsiderate. (*Turning to look at the game.*) Watch the Doctor, he's about to move. Be very careful, old boy, the position is fraught with danger.

HARVESTER (*moving a piece*). I'm going to move my knight.

MAURICE. What would you say if I gave that pawn a little push and murmured check ?

HARVESTER. I should say it was your right, but I should think it a trifle vulgar.

MAURICE. Do you know what I'd do now in your place ?

HARVESTER. No, I don't.

MAURICE. I'd catch my foot in the leg of the table and kick it over accidentally. That's the only way you can save yourself from getting the worst hiding I've ever given you.

HARVESTER (*moving a piece*). Go to the devil.

MAURICE. Oh, you do that, do you ? All right.

(ALICE, *the maid, enters up* R.)

ALICE (*up* R.C.). If you please, ma'am, Major Liconda wants to know if it's too late for him to come in and have a drink.

MAURICE. Of course not. Where is he ?

ALICE. He's at the door, sir.

MRS. TABRET. Ask him to come in.
ALICE. Very good, ma'am.

(She exits.)

MAURICE *(to* HARVESTER*)*. You know him, don't you, old boy ?
HARVESTER. No, I've never met him. He's the fellow who's just taken that furnished house on the golf links, isn't he ?
MRS. TABRET. Yes. I knew him years ago in India. That's why he came here.
MAURICE *(in sly chaff)*. He was one of Mother's numerous admirers. I understand that she treated him very badly.
HARVESTER. I can well believe it. Does he still cherish a hopeless passion for you, Mrs. Tabret ?
MRS. TABRET *(taking the chaff in good part)*. I don't know at all, Dr. Harvester. You'd better ask him.
HARVESTER. Is he a soldier ?
MAURICE. No, he was a policeman. He's just retired. He's a very good chap, and I believe he's rather a good golfer. Colin has played with him two or three times.
MRS. TABRET. I'd asked him to dine to-night, so that Maurice could get a game of bridge, but he couldn't come.

*(*ALICE *enters up* R., *followed by* MAJOR LICONDA.*)*

ALICE. Major Liconda.

(She exits.)

*(*LICONDA *comes down* R.C. *He is a tallish, middle-aged man, with grey hair and a sunburnt face, spare of build, active and alert. He wears a dinner jacket.)*

MRS. TABRET *(shaking hands with him)*. How d'you do ? How very nice of you to look in.
LICONDA. I was on my way home and saw that your lights were on, so I thought I'd just ask if anyone would like to give me a doch-an-dorris.
MRS. TABRET. Help yourself. *(With a gesture of the head.)* The whisky's on the table.
LICONDA *(going to the settee table and pouring himself out a drink)*. Thank you. How are you, Nurse ?
NURSE. How do you do ?
LICONDA. And the patient ?
MAURICE *(lightly)*. Bearing up pretty well, considering all he has to put up with.
LICONDA *(smiling)*. You're in your usual high spirits. *(He moves across towards* MAURICE.*)*
MAURICE. I have much to be thankful for, as the lady said when her husband was run over by a motor bus just after insuring his life.
HARVESTER *(laughing)*. You fool, Maurice.

MRS. TABRET. I don't think you know Dr. Harvester.

(LICONDA *moves* L., *above the table.* HARVESTER *rises. The two men shake hands.*)

HARVESTER. How d'you do ?
LICONDA. Mrs. Tabret tells me you're a very good doctor.
HARVESTER. I take great pains to impress the fact on my patients.
MAURICE. His only serious fault is that he thinks he can play chess.
LICONDA (*crossing back to the settee*). Don't let me disturb your game. (*He sits* L. *of* MRS. TABRET.)
MAURICE. It's finished.
HARVESTER. Not at all. I have three possible moves. (*Making one.*) What do you say to that ?
MAURICE. Mate, you poor fish.
HARVESTER. Damn.
MRS. TABRET. Have you beaten him ?
MAURICE. Hollow.
NURSE (*rising*). Shall I put the chess things away ? (*She turns up and puts her book and bag on the settee table.*)
MAURICE. If you wouldn't mind.

(NURSE WAYLAND *crosses* L.C., *takes the board and the chessmen and puts them away upstage, while the conversation proceeds.*)

LICONDA. I won't keep you up. I'll just swallow my drink and take myself off. I really only came to say I was sorry I couldn't come to dinner.
MAURICE. There's no hurry, you know. I'm not going to bed for hours.
MRS. TABRET. We're really waiting up for Stella and Colin. They've gone to the opera.
LICONDA. I'm a night owl. I never go to bed till I can help it.
MAURICE. You're the man for my money.

(NURSE WAYLAND *moves down* L.C. *to the table.*)

HARVESTER (*rising*). I've got a day's work before me. (*Crossing up* R.C.) I'll just have a drop of Scotch to assuage the pangs of defeat and then I must run. May I ?

(MRS. TABRET *smiles and indicates the table.* HARVESTER *pours himself a drink.*)

MAURICE. Let's send the rest of them off to bed, Major, and have a good old gossip by ourselves.
LICONDA. I'm willing.
MRS. TABRET. If you really want to stay up, Maurice, let Nurse Wayland get you ready and then you'll only just have to slip into bed, and Colin can help you.
MAURICE. All right. What do you say to that, Nurse ?

NURSE (*above the table* L.C.). Well, it's just as you like. I'm quite prepared to stay up until Mrs. Maurice comes in. I'll put you to bed after you've said good night to her.

MAURICE. No, come on. You're looking tired.

MRS. TABRET. You are looking a little peaked, Nurse. I think it's nearly time you had another holiday.

NURSE (*moving to above the invalid bed*). Oh, I don't want a holiday for months.

MAURICE. Put your shoulder to the wheel, Nurse, and gently trundle the wounded hero to his bedchamber.

HARVESTER (*moving to* L. *of the settee*). Shall I come and help ?

MAURICE. Not on your life. It's bad enough to be messed about by one person. I don't want a crowd, damn it.

HARVESTER. Sorry.

MAURICE. I shall only be ten minutes.

(NURSE WAYLAND *wheels out the bed up* L., *and closes the door behind her.* HARVESTER *moves to* R. *of the table* L.C.)

LICONDA. She seems a very nice woman, that nurse.

MRS. TABRET. Yes. She's extremely competent. And I must say she's very gentle and kind. Her patience is really wonderful.

LICONDA. You've had her ever since poor Maurice crashed, haven't you ?

MRS. TABRET. Oh, no. We had three or four before she came. All more or less odious.

HARVESTER (*moving down* L.). She's a rattling good nurse. I think you're lucky to have got her.

MRS. TABRET. I'm sure we are. The only fault I have to find with her is that she's so very reserved. There's nothing come-hither about her. Except for her month's holiday every August she's been with us all day and every day for nearly five years, and I only just know that her name's Beatrice. She calls the boys Mr. Maurice and Mr. Colin, and Stella she calls Mrs. Maurice. She seems to be always a little on her guard. She certainly doesn't encourage familiarity.

HARVESTER. I can't imagine skylarking with her at a Sunday-school treat, I must admit. (*He sits on the armchair* L.C.)

MRS. TABRET. And of course she's a little tactless. It never seems to occur to her that Maurice wants to be alone with his wife. Poor lamb, he has so little. He likes to say good night to Stella the last thing and he likes to say it without anyone looking on. That's why he's staying up now.

LICONDA. Poor old boy.

MRS. TABRET. He can't bear the thought of going to sleep without kissing her. And Nurse Wayland always seems to find something to do just that last moment. He doesn't want to hurt her feelings by sending her out of the room, and he's terrified of being thought sentimental, so he uses every sort of trick and device to get her out of the way.

HARVESTER. But, good Lord, why don't you tell her ? After all, there's no reason why a man shouldn't kiss his wife good night if he wants to.

MRS. TABRET. She's terribly sensitive. Haven't you noticed how often rather tactless people are ? They'll stamp on your toes and then when you tuck them up out of harm's way they're so offended you feel quite miserable about it.

LICONDA. I suppose Maurice is absolutely dependent upon her ?

MRS. TABRET. Absolutely. All sorts of rather unpleasant things have to be done for him, poor dear, and he can't bear that anyone should know about them. Especially Stella.

HARVESTER. Yes, I've discovered that. He doesn't want Stella to have anything to do with his illness.

LICONDA (to HARVESTER, rising and moving R.C.). Is there really no chance of his getting better ?

HARVESTER. I'm afraid not.

(LICONDA moves to the settee table and puts his glass down.)

MRS. TABRET. It's a miracle that he's alive at all.

HARVESTER. He was terribly smashed up, you know. The lower part of his spine was broken and the plane caught fire and he was badly burnt.

LICONDA (crossing down R.C.). It was rotten bad luck.

MRS. TABRET. And when you think that he was flying all through the war and never even had a mishap. It seems so silly that this should happen just when he was trying a new machine. It was so unexpected.

LICONDA. It seems such a pity he didn't stop flying when he married.

MRS. TABRET. It's easy to say that now.

HARVESTER. He was a born flyer. Fellows have told me that he seemed to have a sort of instinct for it.

MRS. TABRET. It was the one thing he was interested in. He wouldn't have given it up for anything in the world. And he was so good at it, it never occurred to me that he could have an accident, he always felt so safe.

LICONDA (sitting L. of MRS. TABRET). I've been told he was absolutely fearless.

HARVESTER. And you know, the strange thing is this, he's just as much interested in it all as he ever was. He follows all the important flights and the tests and so on. If anyone does a new stunt he's full of it.

LICONDA. His courage amazes me. He never seems low or depressed.

MRS. TABRET. Never. His spirits are wonderful. It's one of the most anguishing things I know to see him, when he's in dreadful pain, forcing a joke from his lips.

HARVESTER (rising and taking his glass to the settee table). I'm sorry to think Colin is going away so soon, Mrs. Tabret. I think his being here has done Maurice a lot of good. (*He breaks to* L. *of the settee.*)

MRS. TABRET. When they were boys they were always great friends, and you know brothers aren't always.

LICONDA. They're not, indeed.

(HARVESTER *moves up towards the windows and looks out.*)

MRS. TABRET. And Colin has been away so long. He went to Central America just before Maurice crashed, you know.

LICONDA. Well, has he got to go back ?

MRS. TABRET. He put all his share of his father's money in a coffee plantation and it's doing very well. He loves the life out there and it seems cruel to ask him to give it up to help us to look after his crippled brother.

HARVESTER (*turning from the window*). I think it would be very unfair. (*Crossing to* R. *of the table* L.C.) One has no right to ask anyone to give up his own chance of making the best he can of life.

MRS. TABRET (*with a dry smile*). At all events, with the young one may ask, but the likelihood of their consenting is very slight.

HARVESTER (*at* C.). Not at all, Mrs. Tabret. The country is full of dessicated females who've given up their lives to taking care of an invalid mother.

LICONDA. When I was at Bath a little while ago I saw a good many couples like that, and to tell you the truth I sometimes wondered why the daughters didn't murder their mothers.

HARVESTER. They often do. Every doctor will tell you that he's had a case where he has a strong suspicion that some old woman who lived too long has been poisoned by her relatives. But he takes jolly good care not to say anything about it.

LICONDA. Why ?

HARVESTER (*moving towards the* L. *end of the settee*). Oh, it's rotten for a man's practice. Nothing can do you so much damage as to be mixed up in a murder case.

MRS. TABRET. I've often pondered over the problem of the woman like myself. I'm not sure if the best way of dealing with us wouldn't be to do as some African tribes do. At a certain age take us to the river's brim and push us gently but firmly in.

LICONDA (*with a smile*). What happens if they swim ?

MRS. TABRET. The family is prepared for that. They stand on the banks with brickbats and take pot shots at their struggling but aged grandmother. It discourages her efforts to get out.

(NURSE WAYLAND *opens the door up* L. HARVESTER *crosses, and helps her to wheel back the bed on which* MAURICE *is lying to* R. *of the table* L.C.)

MAURICE (*as he is wheeled down*). Here we are again. I'm all fixed up and ready for any excitement. What about a tune on the gramophone ?

HARVESTER (R. *of* MAURICE). I must go.

MRS. TABRET. And Nurse Wayland should go to bed.

NURSE (*crossing* R. *to the settee table*). I'll just gather my things together and say good night. (*Picking up her bag and book.*) Are you sure Mrs. Maurice and your brother won't go and have supper after the opera ? (*She comes to* L. *of the settee table.*)

MAURICE. I'm sure they will. I particularly told Stella she was to have a real bust. It's not often she goes on the loose, poor dear.

NURSE. Then they won't be home till four.

MAURICE. Does that mean you disapprove of my staying up, you hard and brutal woman ?

NURSE. Doesn't Dr. Harvester ?

HARVESTER. Very much. (*Moving down stage and to* L.) But I'm aware that Maurice has no intention of going to sleep till he knows his wife is safely home again, and my theory is that it does people good now and then to do what they shouldn't. (*He turns at the chair down* L.)

LICONDA. That is the kind of doctor for me.

MAURICE (*pricking up his ears*). What's that ?

MRS. TABRET. What, Maurice ?

MAURICE. I thought I heard a car. Yes, by jove. It's Stella. I'd know the sound of that car in a thousand.

(*Now the sound of a car driving up is almost distinct.*)

LICONDA. Do you mean to say you can hear from this distance ?

MAURICE. You bet your life I can. That's the family bus. Now just stay a minute and see Stella, Doctor. She's got her best bib and tucker on and she's a sight for sore eyes.

LICONDA. What were they giving at the opera to-night ?

MAURICE. *Tristan.* That's why I insisted on Stella going. It was after *Tristan* that we got engaged. D'you remember, Mother ?

MRS. TABRET. Of course I do.

MAURICE. We'd all been to hear it and then we went on to supper. I drove Stella round Regent's Park in a little two-seater I had then and I swore I'd go on driving round and round till she promised to marry me. *Tristan* had given her such an appetite that by the time we were half-way around the second time, she said, oh, hell, if I must either marry you or die of starvation I'd sooner marry you.

HARVESTER. Is there a word of truth in this story, Mrs. Tabret ?

MRS. TABRET. I don't know. They were both as mad as hatters in those days. All I know is that the rest of us had only just ordered our supper when they came in looking like a pair of cats who'd swallowed a canary and said they were engaged.

(*The door up* R. *is opened and* STELLA *enters, followed by her brother-in-law,* COLIN TABRET. STELLA *is twenty-eight and beautiful. She is wearing an evening dress and an opera cloak.* COLIN, *a tall, dark, handsome fellow in the early thirties, is in full evening dress, long coat and white tie.* LICONDA *and* HARVESTER *have risen at* STELLA'S *entrance.*)

MAURICE. Stella !
STELLA. Darling ! Have you missed me ?

(*She crosses down to him and lightly kisses him on the forehead.* COLIN *crosses above the table to* L., *and speaks with* HARVESTER.)

MAURICE. Why are you back already, you wretched girl ? You promised me to go and have supper.
STELLA. I was so thrilled and excited by the opera. I felt I simply couldn't eat a thing. (*She crosses to the settee, smiles at* LICONDA, *shakes hands and puts her bag and gloves on the* L. *arm of the settee.*)
MAURICE (*during this business*). Hang it all, you might have gone to Lucien's and had a dance or two and a bottle of champagne. What's the good of my spending the eyes of my head on buying you a new dress when you won't let anyone see it. (*To* LICONDA.) She said it was too dressed up to go to the opera in, but I exercised my marital authority and made her.

(LICONDA *sits again.*)

STELLA (*moving a little from the settee*). Darling, I wanted to show it off in the intervals, but I hadn't the nerve and I kept my cloak on.
MAURICE. Well, take it off now and show the gentlemen. The only way I managed to get them to stay was by promising to let them have a look at your new dress when you came home.
STELLA (*crossing below the bed to* L. *of it*). What nonsense. As if Major Liconda or Dr. Harvester knew one frock from another. (*She sits on the end of the bed.*)
MAURICE. Don't be so damned contemptuous of the male sex, Stella. Take off your cloak and let's have a good look at you.
STELLA. You brute, Maurice, you've made me feel shy now. (*She slips off her cloak.*)
MAURICE. Stand up.

(STELLA *hesitates a moment and then, still holding the cloak about her hips, stands and moves a little* L. *She lets the cloak fall to her feet.*)

HARVESTER (*who has moved down* L. *a little*). It's lovely.

(STELLA *staggers a little and smothers a cry.*)

MAURICE. Halloa, what's the matter ?

(COLIN *catches* STELLA *and helps her to the armchair.* NURSE WAYLAND *crosses to her quickly.*)

STELLA. It's nothing. I feel so frightfully faint.

(HARVESTER *goes to* STELLA, COLIN *making way for him. At the same time,* MRS. TABRET *rises, with* LICONDA, *and they move to* R.C.)

MRS. TABRET (*as she rises*). Oh, my dear !

MAURICE. Stella !

HARVESTER (L. *of* STELLA). It's all right, Maurice. Don't fuss. (*To* STELLA.) Put your head down between your knees.

(*He puts his hand on her neck to force her head down.* NURSE WAYLAND *puts her hands to her side as though to support her. But* STELLA *pushes her away.*)

STELLA. No, don't. Don't come near me. , I shall be all right again in a minute. It's silly of me.

MAURICE. I'm sorry, darling. It was my fault.

STELLA. It's nothing. I feel better already.

MRS. TABRET (*moving to above and* R. *of* MAURICE'S *bed*). My own belief is that she's just faint from lack of food. At what time did you dine ?

COLIN (*now above the table* L.C.). We didn't dine.

MRS. TABRET. Oh, you *are* a ridiculous pair !

STELLA. I'm really quite all right now.

MRS. TABRET. Nurse, would you mind going to the kitchen and seeing if you can find anything for these silly young things to eat ?

NURSE. Of course not. (*Crossing to up* R.) There ought to be some ham. I'll make them some sandwiches.

(*She exits up* R.)

MRS. TABRET. Colin can get a bottle of champagne out of the cellar.

COLIN. All right, Mother. (*He crosses to up* R., *and turns.*) Is there any ice in the house ? I've got a thirst I wouldn't sell for twenty pounds.

(*He exits* R.)

LICONDA (*moving down* R.C.). Well, I'll say good-bye. (*To* STELLA.) I'm sorry you're feeling poorly.

STELLA. I shall be all right when I've had something to eat. I think Mrs. Tabret is quite right. What I want is a large ham sandwich with a lot of mustard on it.

MAURICE. You're looking better, you know. Just for a moment you were as white as a sheet.

LICONDA (*to* MRS. TABRET). Good-bye.

MRS. TABRET (*moving up* R. *with* LICONDA *to the door*). Good-bye. It was so nice of you to look in.

(*Exit* LICONDA.)

(MRS. TABRET *moves down above the table* L.C.)

HARVESTER (L. *of the armchair*). I'll just stay a moment or two longer if you don't mind. I don't trust these young women who don't feed themselves properly.

(MRS. TABRET *gives* MAURICE *and* STELLA *a glance. She knows they want to have a moment to themselves.*)

MRS. TABRET (*to* DR. HARVESTER). Let's take a turn in the garden, shall we ? It's so warm and lovely.

HARVESTER. Come on. (*They move up to the french windows.*) And I hope Nurse Wayland has the sense to cut a sandwich for me, too.

(*The* DOCTOR *and* MRS. TABRET *go out.*)

(*As soon as they are alone* STELLA *goes over to* L. *of* MAURICE'S *bed and gives him a long, loving kiss on the lips. He puts his arm round her neck.*)

MAURICE. Darling.

(*She releases herself and sitting down on the bed holds one of his thin, sick hands.*)

STELLA. I'm sorry I made such a fool of myself.

MAURICE. You scared the life out of me, you little beast. Why didn't you go on to some place and have a bite before you came home ?

STELLA (*rising*). I didn't want to. (*Crossing to the settee.*) I wanted to get back. (*She puts her cloak on the settee.*)

MAURICE. Will you give me your word of honour that you didn't go on to dance because you thought I should be waiting up for you ?

STELLA (*crossing to above the bed*). Don't be an old silly. (*Putting a hand on his shoulder.*) You know that I love to think you want me back so much. (*Moving above the table and down* L. *of the armchair.*) You don't imagine I care a hang about dancing.

MAURICE. You little liar. How can anyone dance as well as you without being crazy about it ? You're the best dancer I ever danced with.

STELLA (*sitting on the* R. *arm of the armchair*). Oh, but you know how one changes. All the dances are different now, and after all I'm not so young as I was either.

MAURICE. You're twenty-eight. You're only a girl. You ought to be having the time of your life. Oh, my dear, it is rotten for you.

STELLA. Oh, darling, don't. You mustn't think that. Don't imagine for a moment that I've given up a thing that meant anything to me.

MAURICE. You must allow me to have my own opinion. Anyhow it's been a snip having old Colin here. It's damned well forced you to go out.

STELLA. Darling, you talk as though I was shut up like a nun. I'm always going out. I see all the plays.

MAURICE. Yes, at matinees with my mother. She's a dear old thing, but she's not precisely exhilarating. After all, when one's young one wants to be with young people. One wants to say and do all sorts of things that seem merely silly to the elderly. They smile indulgently because they have the tolerance of wise old people. Damn it all, one doesn't want their indulgence. One wants to play the fool because one's young. And it's wise for the young to be rather foolish.

STELLA. My dear, you mustn't be epigrammatic. They tell me it's so out of date.

MAURICE. I was hoping you'd dance till your feet were dropping off and then go for a spin in the moonlight. Do you remember, we did that once one night and we had breakfast at a pub on the river in our evening things ? It was fun, wasn't it ?

STELLA (*rising and moving to* R.C.). We were a pair of lunatics in those days. (*Turning.*) I was much too tired to do anything like that. I only wanted to get home.

MAURICE. The honest fact is that you've lost the habit of going on a binge.

STELLA (*moving to* R. *of the bed*). I don't want to go on a binge if you can't come with me.

MAURICE. That is perfectly idiotic of you, my poor child. I wish that silly ass Colin weren't going away so soon.

STELLA (*moving away to the* L. *end of the settee*). He only came home for six months and he's stayed nearly a year.

MAURICE. You promised you'd try to persuade him to stay on for a bit.

STELLA (*fidgeting with the contents of her bag*). He must get back to his work.

MAURICE. Why can't he sell his old plantation and settle down here ?

STELLA (*picking up her cloak and moving to the french windows*). He'd be a fish out of water in England. (*She stands at the windows, her cloak draped on her* L. *shoulder.*) When a man's got used to the sort of life he's lived out there it's frightfully difficult for him to settle down in an office or something like that.

MAURICE. I suppose it is really. I should have hated it, too. I wasn't really thinking of myself, and Mother must be used to having a pair of useless sons by now. I was thinking of you.

STELLA (*speaking into the room*). I'm quite capable of thinking of myself, darling. I'm a very selfish woman.

MAURICE. My poor child, you mustn't think because I've got a broken back I'm a drivelling imbecile.

STELLA (*crossing down to above the bed*). How can I think anything else when I see you fussing because you imagine I may be having a rather thin time ? I'm not having a rather thin time. You never try to prevent me from doing anything I want to. I don't know what it is to be bored. Why, I haven't time for half the things I want to do.

MAURICE. Yes, you're wonderful . . . You've always been wonderful. You've made the best of a bad job, all right. I've had to. But why should you ? Resignation. I've had to set my teeth and learn it. But what has a girl like you to do with resignation ?

STELLA (*behind* MAURICE, *her arms round his neck*). Oh, darling, don't talk like that. You mustn't think such things. I married you because I loved you. What a foul brute I should be if I stopped loving you now that you need my love more than ever.

MAURICE. Oh, my dear, we can't love because we ought to. Love comes and goes and we can none of us help ourselves.

STELLA (*disengaging and moving down* R. *of the bed*). Maurice, what do you mean ? (*She looks away.*) Has there been anything in my behaviour to lead you to think that I wasn't the same as I'd always been ?

MAURICE (*with deep affection*). No, darling. You've been angelic always, always. (*Taken aback.*) Why, what's the matter ? You suddenly went quite pale. You're not feeling faint again ?

STELLA. No. (*Moving to the settee.*) I'm all right.

MAURICE. You know, if I've seemed often to take for granted all you've done for me you mustn't think I'm not conscious all the time how much I owe you.

STELLA. That's very silly of you, my pet. (*Easing a little towards him.*) I don't know that I've done anything for you at all except be moderately civil. You've never let me.

MAURICE. I've never let you nurse me. Not on your life. I couldn't have borne that you should have anything to do with the disgusting side of illness, my precious. I'm so grateful to you, Stella. (*He holds out his hand to her.*)

(STELLA *moves close to the* R. *side of the bed. A pause.*)

MAURICE (*casually*). You know that I'm never going to get well, Stella, don't you ?

STELLA. I don't indeed. It's a long business, we know that, but I'm absolutely convinced you'll get at all events very much better.

MAURICE. They tell me that one of these days they'll try operating again to see if they can't possibly put me right. But I know they're lying. They pretend they can do something in order to give me hope, and I pretend to believe them because it's the easiest thing to do. I know I'm here for life, Stella.

(*There is a moment's pause. This is the first time that* STELLA *has realised that* MAURICE *knows his case is hopeless.*)

STELLA (*very earnestly, leaning over the bed, left arm round his neck*). Then let's take what comfort we can in the great joy we've had in one another in the days when you were well and strong. I shall always be grateful for the happiness you gave me and for your love.

MAURICE. Do you think that's changed ? No. I love you as deeply, as devotedly as I ever did. I'm not often silly and sentimental, am I, Stella ?

(*He puts his right hand up towards her and she takes it.*)

STELLA (*with a little smile*). Is it so silly to be sentimental ? (*Straightening up.*) No, you're not often.

MAURICE. You're everything in the world to me, Stella. People have been most awfully kind to me, and it's not till you're crocked up as I am that you find out how kind people are. They've been simply topping. But there's not one of them that I wouldn't see in hell if it would save you from unhappiness or trouble.

STELLA (*in a lighter, chaffing tone, fetching the stool near the settee table*). Well, I wouldn't tell them if I were you. I don't believe they'd awfully like it. (*She brings the stool to* R. *of the bed*.)

MAURICE (*with a smile, as* STELLA *sits*). I ought to be frightened because I'm so dependent on you, but I'm not because I know, not just with my mind or my heart, but with every nerve in me, with every little feeling and every pain, how good you are.

STELLA (*trying to take his speech lightly*). Now, darling, you really are exaggerating. If you go on like this I shall send you to bed.

MAURICE. My precious. You can laugh at me, but I see the tears in your eyes.

STELLA (*with sudden emotion*). Maurice, I'm a very weak, a very imperfect, and a very sinful woman.

MAURICE (*suddenly changing, but still with the greatest affection*). Come down to earth, you silly little ass.

STELLA (*unable not to feel a trifle anxious*). Why are you saying all this to me just to-night ?

MAURICE (*smiling*). One can't always jump through a hoop to make people laugh. It's hardly becoming in a gentleman approaching middle age who's chained to an invalid bed. You must forgive me if my flow of jokes sometimes runs dry.

STELLA. You're sure you're not worrying about anything ?

MAURICE. You know, when you're shut up as I am you find out all sorts of interesting things. Being an invalid fortunately has its compensations. Of course, people are very sympathetic, but you mustn't abuse their sympathy. They ask you how you are, but they don't really care a damn. Why should they ? Life is for the living and I'm dead.

STELLA (*strangely harassed*). Maurice, oh, my darling.

MAURICE. You must take care not to bore the people who come to see you and you soon discover that it bores them if you talk about yourself. Let them talk about themselves. That always interests them and they say, what an intelligent fellow he is. Make jokes. Make all the jokes you can—good, bad, and indifferent : when you've made them laugh, they feel they needn't be sorry for you, and that's a relief to them. And when they go away they feel so kindly disposed towards you.

STELLA. Oh, my darling, you break my heart. It's so cruel to think that you should have had to learn such bitter truths.

MAURICE. My dear, they're not so bitter as all that. I should never have mentioned it only I wanted to tell you that it's you who've given me the courage to carry on. I'm not unhappy. I don't know how many years I shall hang on, but if you'll help me, darling, I think I can make a pretty good job of it. I owe everything to you.

Nothing matters to me very much when I know I shall see you to-morrow and the next day and the day after that and always.

STELLA (*shattered by emotion*). Maurice, I'm unworthy of such love. I'm so ashamed. I'm so selfish. I'm so thoughtless.

MAURICE. Never.

STELLA (*rising*). Why did you make me go out to-night ? (*She turns up* R.C.) Did you think it was any pleasure to me ? (*She moves to the head of the bed.*)

MAURICE. I didn't care. I was thinking of my pleasure. I wanted you to hear again the music we'd heard together that night we got engaged. I was crazy about you. Do you remember how you cried in the second act when Tristan and Isolde sing that duet of theirs and I held your hand in the dark ? Why did you cry ?

(STELLA *goes to the settee table for the handkerchief in her bag.*)

STELLA (*wiping her eyes*). I cried because I loved you and I was happy.

MAURICE. Did you cry to-night ?

STELLA. I don't know.

MAURICE. You know, that music is stunning, isn't it ?

STELLA (*nodding and smiling through her tears*). People seem to think it's above the average. (*She moves to* L. *of the settee.*)

MAURICE. You seemed to carry it still in your eyes when you came in. They were bright and shining. You've never looked so beautiful as you looked to-night.

STELLA (*recovered now and chaffing him again as she sits on the settee*). Go on, darling, I can bear much more in the same strain.

MAURICE. I could go on for weeks.

STELLA. No, then I'd be afraid you were prejudiced. Go on till the sandwiches come in.

MAURICE. Give me your hands.

STELLA. No, I won't. Let's be sensible and talk about other things.

MAURICE. Of course, the honest-to-God truth is that you're ever so much lovelier than when I married you. What is there that gives you this sudden new radiance ?

STELLA. I don't know why I should look any different from usual.

MAURICE. I watch your face. I know every change in it from day to day. A year ago you had a strained, almost a hunted, look, but now lately you've had an air that is strangely peaceful. You've gained a sort of beautiful serenity.

STELLA (*chaffing*). My poor lamb. I'm afraid that can only be due to advancing years. Soon you'll discover the first wrinkle on my forehead and then the first white hair.

MAURICE. No, no. You must never grow old. I couldn't bear it. Oh, how cruel that all that beauty . . .

STELLA (*rising, interrupting him quickly*). No, don't, Maurice, please ! (*She crosses to him*).

MAURICE. It would have been better for both of us if I'd been killed when I crashed. I'm no use to you, I'm no use to anybody.

STELLA (*to* R. *of the head of the bed*). Oh, Maurice, how *can* you say that ? Don't you know how desperately afraid I was when they told me you were hurt and how relieved, how infinitely thankful when they told me at last, after days and days of anguish, that you would live ?

MAURICE. They should never have let me. Why didn't they put me out of my misery when I was all smashed up ? It only wanted an injection a little stronger than usual. That was the cruelty— to bring me back to life. Cruel to me and ten times more cruel to you.

STELLA (*close to him, her hand on his shoulder*). I won't let you say it. It's not true. It's not true.

MAURICE. I think I could have borne it if we'd had a child. Oh, Stella, if we'd only had a little kid and I could think to myself that it was you and me. And you would have something to console you. After all, it's a woman's destiny to have children. You wouldn't have felt that you had entirely wasted your life.

STELLA (*moving down and sitting by him on the stool*). But, Maurice, my dear, I *don't* feel I've wasted my life. You're not yourself to-night. You're ill and tired. Oh, what has come over you ?

MAURICE. I love you, Stella. I want to take you in my arms as I used to. I want to press my lips to yours and see your eyes close and your head fall back and feel your dear soft body grow tense . . . Stella, Stella. I can't bear it. (*He bursts into tears, clinging to her.*)

STELLA. Maurice, darling. Don't. Don't cry.

(*He sobs hysterically while she rocks him to and fro like a mother her child. Then he gets hold of himself.*)

MAURICE (*with a complete change of tone, in a matter-of-fact voice*). Oh, my God, what a damned fool I am. Give me a hand-kerchief.

(*She gives him one from under the pillow and he blows his nose.*)

STELLA. My dear, you did frighten me.

MAURICE. It's what they call a nerve storm. It's lucky it was only you here. It would have been a pretty kettle of fish if Nurse Wayland had seen me like that.

STELLA (*trying to laugh with him*). It would have been a much prettier kettle of fish if I'd seen you clinging to her.

MAURICE. I say, you haven't got a glass, have you ?

STELLA (*rising and crossing to the settee*). My angel, how do you imagine I apply lipstick ?

(*She takes a little glass out of her bag and brings it to him.*)

MAURICE (*laughing at himself*). I *do* look rather tear-stained, if I may say so. (*He wipes his eyes with the handkerchief.*)

STELLA (*moving* R. *to the settee*). Let me powder your nose. You can't think what a comfort it is after you've been upset.

MAURICE. Go on with you. You can give me a whisky and soda if you like.

STELLA. All right. But I'll powder mine. (*She takes out her powder compact.*)

MAURICE. I feel like a house on fire now.

STELLA (*business with puff*). I wish someone would explain how it is that a dab of powder can in the twinkling of an eye reduce a woman's nose from an unwieldy lump to a dear little thing that no one can deny is her best feature.

MAURICE. These are the miracles of science that we read about.

STELLA (*turning up to the settee table*). Now I'll get you your whisky and soda.

(COLIN *comes in with a tray on which are glasses, ice, and a bottle of champagne.*)

MAURICE. Here's Colin. I'll have a glass of champagne instead.

COLIN (*carrying the tray to the table* L.C.). I'm afraid I've been a devil of a time.

MAURICE. I knew you couldn't be trusted in the cellar by yourself. We were just going to send a search party after you.

COLIN. Well, first I couldn't find anything to break the ice with and then I couldn't find the nippers to cut the wire. And then I thought I might as well put the car away. I didn't want to leave it outside all night.

MAURICE. Meanwhile Stella is famishing.

COLIN. Nurse Wayland is just coming. She's making some sandwiches with bacon and they smell a fair treat.

(NURSE WAYLAND *enters up* R., *with a covered entree dish.*)

STELLA. Here she is. That is kind of you, Nurse. If there's anything I adore it's bacon sandwiches.

NURSE (*carrying the dish to the table* L.C.). I haven't brought any knives and forks. I thought you could eat with your fingers.

STELLA. Heavenly.

COLIN. I'll just bolt up and change my coat. I might just as well be comfortable and I shan't be a minute.

STELLA. Well, I'm not going to wait for you.

COLIN. All right. Go right ahead. (*Crossing to the door up* R.) But leave me my fair share or else all is over between us.

(*He exits up* R.)

(STELLA *goes to the window and calls into the garden.*)

STELLA. Dr. Harvester, come and eat a sandwich before it gets cold.

(NURSE WAYLAND *crosses to* R. *of the bed.*)

MAURICE. I don't think I'll wait to see you people make pigs of yourselves. I think I'll turn in.

STELLA (*moving down to the table* L.C.). Aren't you going to have a drink with us ? (*She is about to pour a glass of wine.*)

MAURICE. I don't think I will if you don't mind. I'm rather tired.

STELLA (*putting down the bottle*). Oh, I am sorry, Maurice. But there's nothing to stay up for if you're tired.

MAURICE. You might look in on your way up to bed, Stella.

(NURSE WAYLAND *turns the bed to wheel it out.*)

STELLA. Yes, rather. But I shan't disturb you if you're asleep.

MAURICE. I shan't be asleep. I've got a bit of a head. I'll just lie still in the dark and it'll go away.

(*As* NURSE WAYLAND *starts to wheel* MAURICE *out,* MRS. TABRET *and* DR. HARVESTER *come in and move down* R.C.)

HARVESTER. Did I hear you calling me ?

STELLA. You did. Maurice is going to bed.

MRS. TABRET. Oh, I'm glad. (*Above* MAURICE'S *bed.*) It's fearfully late. Good night, old boy. Sleep well. (*She leans over and kisses him on the forehead.*)

MAURICE. Good night, Mother. Bless you.

HARVESTER (*crossing to the bed*). Let me give you a hand, Nurse.

NURSE. I can manage perfectly. I'm so used to wheeling the invalid bed and he weighs nothing.

MAURICE. I never weighed more than ten stone eight when I was well.

HARVESTER. Never mind. Let me push him in. I'd like to.

MAURICE. Let the man do something for his money, Nurse. (*Putting on a Cockney accent.*) You bring me drops and me powder puff, dearie.

(*The* NURSE *goes up* L. *and opens the door, and* DR. HARVESTER *pushes the bed out.*)

STELLA. Don't be long, Doctor, or the sandwiches will be stone cold.

(*The* NURSE *follows* HARVESTER *off and the door is closed.* STELLA *and* MRS. TABRET *are left alone.*)

Maurice is rather nervous to-night.

MRS. TABRET (*moving towards* R.C.). Yes, I noticed it.

STELLA. I'm sorry I went to the opera.

MRS. TABRET (*turning at* R.C.). My dear, you go out so little.

STELLA (*moving down* L. *of the armchair*). I haven't the inclination really.

MRS. TABRET. I'm afraid you're awfully tired.

STELLA (*with a smile*). Dead. (*She sits in the armchair.*)

MRS. TABRET. Why don't you eat something ?

STELLA. No, I'll wait till the others come. (*She sits back, relaxing with her eyes closed.*)

(*A pause.*)

MRS. TABRET (*moving down below the settee*). Whatever happens, darling, I want you to know that I'm deeply grateful for all you've done for Maurice.

STELLA (*opening her eyes and sitting up, startled*). Why do you say that ? You don't think he's any worse ?

MRS. TABRET (*picking up her needlework and bag from the settee*). No, I think he's just about the same as usual.

STELLA. He does get a little nervous and highly-strung sometimes.

MRS. TABRET. Yes, I know.

STELLA. You startled me. I don't know why you should suddenly say a thing like that.

MRS. TABRET (*moving to* C., *smiling*). Is there any reason I shouldn't ?

STELLA. It sounded strangely ominous.

MRS. TABRET. I feel I'd like you to know that I realise what a great sacrifice you've made for him for so many years. You mustn't think that I've taken it as a matter of course.

STELLA (*rising and going to* MRS. TABRET). Oh, my dear, don't, don't. If there was anything I could do to make things a little easier for him I was anxious to do it.

MRS. TABRET. After all, you didn't marry him to be the help-mate of a helpless cripple.

STELLA. One takes the rough with the smooth.

MRS. TABRET. I know it's very irksome to have an old woman like me always living with you. It's difficult to be a mother-in-law and welcome.

STELLA (*charmingly, taking* MRS. TABRET'S *hands*). My dear, you've been kindness itself to me. What should I have done without you ?

MRS. TABRET. I will admit that I've tried not to be a pest. You'd have been within your rights if you'd refused to have me to live here. I must thank you for all you've done for me, too.

STELLA. Oh, my dear, you make me feel quite shy. (*She crosses* MRS. TABRET *to the settee and sits.*)

MRS. TABRET (*turning to look at* STELLA). You're a young and very beautiful woman. You have the right to live your life just as everyone else has. (*Moving to the settee.*) For four years now you've given up everything to be the sole comfort of a man who was your husband only because a legal ceremony had joined you together. (*She sits* L. *of* STELLA.)

STELLA. No, no. Because love had joined us together.

MRS. TABRET (*putting her hand over* STELLA'S). My poor child, I'm so desperately sorry for you. Whatever the future may have in store I shall never forget your courage, your self-sacrifice, and your patience.

STELLA (*puzzled and a little frightened*). I don't understand what you mean.

MRS. TABRET (*with a tolerant and ironic smile*). Don't you? Well, let us suppose that this is the anniversary of my wedding-day and my thoughts have been much occupied with the ups and downs, the fortunes and misfortunes of married life.

(COLIN *re-enters up* R. *He has taken off his long evening coat and wears a very shabby old golf coat.*)

COLIN (*crossing to the table* L.C.). Hulloa, where are the others?
STELLA. Maurice has gone to bed. Dr. Harvester is just coming.
MRS. TABRET. Now, come on, children. Sit down and have something to eat.

(STELLA *rises and crosses to the table* L.C.)

COLIN. I'll pour out some wine, shall I?

(*He pours out three glasses of champagne while* STELLA *helps herself to a sandwich.*)

STELLA. Hm. Scrumptious. (*She offers the dish to* COLIN *and then takes it and a glass of champagne to* MRS. TABRET.)
MRS. TABRET (*taking the glass but not a sandwich*). Nurse Wayland makes them well, doesn't she?
STELLA. Marvellously.

(DR. HARVESTER *comes in.*)

(*Crossing to the table with the dish.*) If you don't hurry up you'll be too late. They're simply lovely.

HARVESTER (R. *of* STELLA). I'll just have a sandwich and swallow one glass, and bolt. It's any old time, and I've got to be up bright and early in the morning.

(STELLA *hands him the sandwiches and a glass of wine. He takes a sandwich and the glass and moves* R.C.)

COLIN (*moving down* L. *of the table*). Is Maurice all right?
HARVESTER. Oh, fairly. He's a bit down to-night for some reason—I don't know why. He was in great spirits earlier in the evening. (*He begins to eat his sandwich.*)

(STELLA *draws the stool nearer the table and sits.*)

MRS. TABRET. I expect he's tired. He *would* sit up.
HARVESTER (*by the* L. *end of the settee*). Nurse Wayland says that something has upset him. Is that true?
MRS. TABRET. Not that I know of.

(COLIN *sits in the armchair* L. *of the table.*)

HARVESTER. He says he's got a headache. I've left him a sleeping draught that he can take if he can't get off or wakes in the night and feels restless.

STELLA. I'll go in and see him before I go to bed. If he can only get a good rest I'm sure he'll be his usual self to-morrow.

MRS. TABRET. Sit with him a little, Stella.

STELLA. Of course I will.

HARVESTER (*putting his glass on the settee table*). Well, I must be off. Good night, Mrs. Tabret. I've had a jolly evening.

MRS. TABRET (*putting her glass on the settee table, and rising*). I'll come and see you to the door and then I shall go up to bed. (*Crossing to* STELLA.) Good night, children.

STELLA (*rising*). Good night.

(*They kiss one another and then* MRS. TABRET *crosses and kisses* COLIN, *who has risen.*)

MRS. TABRET. Good night, Colin dear. Don't stay up too late, either of you.

COLIN. And put out the lights and see that the windows are properly closed and the safety catches in place. I will, Mother.

MRS. TABRET (*pleased with his chaff, to* DR. HARVESTER). You see how these boys treat me. They have no respect for their aged mother.

COLIN. A certain amount of restrained affection, however.

MRS. TABRET (*turning up* R.C.). Bless you, my dear, now and always.

HARVESTER. Good night. (*He goes to the door up* R.)

STELLA. Good night. We shall see you in a day or two, I suppose.

HARVESTER (*opening the door for* MRS. TABRET). I expect so.

COLIN. Good night, old boy.

(DR. HARVESTER *and* MRS. TABRET *exit up* R.)

(COLIN *goes up to the french windows, shuts them, and draws the curtains. The moment the door closes on* MRS. TABRET, STELLA *puts down the sandwich she has been making a pretence of eating. She stands looking out into space. When* COLIN *has finished closing up, he turns out most of the lights by the switch at the* R. *door, moves down* R. *and puts out the floor standard lamp. The room is now shrouded in darkness and there is only light on* STELLA. COLIN *moves in to below the settee.*)

COLIN. Stella . . . Stella . . .

(*She gives a stifled sob and looks at him, misery in her eyes.*)

STELLA (*sinking on to the stool*). Oh, Colin.

COLIN (*going towards her*). My poor child.

STELLA (*rising*). Don't touch me. (*Moving to down* L.C.) Oh, what shall I do ? (*Turning at* L.C.) Colin, what have we done ?

COLIN. Darling.

STELLA.   Maurice was so strange to-night. I couldn't make him out. I was almost afraid he suspected.

COLIN (*at* R.C.).   Impossible.

STELLA.   He must never kno͠w. Never ! I'd do anything in the world to prevent it.

COLIN.   I'm so terribly sorry.

STELLA.   We're in a hopeless pass. Hopeless. Why did you ever love me ? Why did I ever love you ?

COLIN.   Stella.

(*He moves a pace towards her, stretching out his arms, but she turns away.*)

STELLA.   Oh, I'm so ashamed. (*She hides her face with her hands.*)

CURTAIN

ACT II

SCENE.—The same. Next morning, and about midday.

The easy chair which was below the settee is now R. *of the table* L.C.
COLIN *is seated at the writing desk* L., *writing letters.* MAJOR
LICONDA *is shown in up* R., *by* ALICE. *He is in golfing attire.*

ALICE. Major Liconda.

(She exits.)

(COLIN *rises, and goes to meet* LICONDA, *who comes down* R.C.)

COLIN. Oh, how do you do ?

(They shake hands.)

LICONDA. My dear boy, what an awful thing. I'm absolutely
horrified. I've only just this minute heard.

COLIN. It's nice of you to have come. As you can imagine
we're all very much upset.

LICONDA (*moving down* R.C., *below the settee*). I've been playing
golf. I went out early. I had a match at nine. Someone told me
at the clubhouse when I got in. I could hardly believe it. (*He sits.*)

COLIN (*who has moved down a little,* C.). I'm afraid it's true all
the same.

LICONDA. But Maurice seemed comparatively well last night.

COLIN. Anyhow, no worse than usual.

LICONDA. I thought him in such good spirits. He was full of
fun. He was cracking jokes.

COLIN. Yes, I know. (*He moves down* L.C., *and turns.*)

LICONDA. Of course, I know nothing. You know Blake at the
club ? I don't know if you've ever played with him.

COLIN (*moving up* C. *again*). No. But I've met him.

LICONDA. Well, he came up when I was standing at the bar
having a drink and said to me : " I say, have you heard that poor
Maurice Tabret died last night ? " By George, it gave me a shock.
You know, when one isn't as young as one was, it always gives one
a turn to hear of the death of someone you knew.

COLIN. I suppose it does.

LICONDA. Blake hadn't heard any of the details. Was he taken
suddenly worse in the night ?

COLIN. No, he said he was rather tired. Stella and I were going
to have a snack before going to bed. He said he wouldn't wait. It
was very natural ; it was getting a bit late you know. Harvester
was here and he went along with him and Nurse Wayland and
helped to put him to bed. He seemed all right then.

LICONDA. Did he just die in his sleep ?

COLIN. I suppose so.

LICONDA. That's the best way, isn't it ? We'd all give something to know for certain that when our time came we'd pass out like that.

COLIN. He can't have felt ill, or he'd have rung. He had a bell-push under his pillow and it rings in Nurse Wayland's room. She'd have been down like a flash if there'd been a sound.

LICONDA. She heard nothing ?

COLIN. Nothing.

LICONDA. When did you find out, then ?

COLIN. Well, you see, sometimes, if he'd had a poorish night, you know, he slept rather late in the morning. And he was always allowed to sleep on. You know what nurses are. However rotten a night you've had, you must be washed and have your hair brushed and your pillows shaken.

LICONDA. Don't I know it !

COLIN. Well, Stella stopped all that. She insisted that no one should go in to Maurice till he rang.

LICONDA. Poor devil, at all events when he was asleep he was happy.

COLIN. I believe it was the only matter on which there'd been any friction between Stella and Nurse Wayland. Stella said she didn't want to interfere with anything else, but on that point she insisted. And Nurse Wayland could either knuckle under or go.

LICONDA. Quite right.

COLIN (sitting in the easy chair C.) . We were just finishing breakfast when Nurse Wayland came in. I noticed she was very white. She said she'd just been in to Maurice. Then Stella got right up on her hind legs. "I won't have it," she said, "I've forbidden you to go in till he rings. How dare you disobey me." I've never seen Stella in such a passion. I saw that Nurse Wayland was trembling. She looked all funny. Scared, you know. But not of Stella. I had a sort of suspicion something was wrong. " Is anything the matter, Nurse ? " I asked. She gave a sort of cry and clenched her hands. " I'm afraid he's dead," she said.

LICONDA. Good God ! How awful.

COLIN. Stella gave a sort of gasp and then she went into a dead faint.

LICONDA. Your poor Mother.

COLIN (rising). Mother was wonderful. (He moves up C. and then turns.) I sprang forward to help Stella. She'd fallen on the floor—for a moment I was afraid the shock had killed her. And I saw Mother sitting at the table with a piece of toast in her hand. She just looked at Nurse Wayland, I don't know, as though she couldn't understand. She was awfully white, and then she began to tremble. She never made a sound. She shrank back into her chair and seemed all of a sudden to become an old, old woman.

LICONDA. Why didn't the fool break it to you more gently ?

COLIN. Then Mother stood up. She got hold of herself quicker than any of us. I never knew she had such nerve.

LICONDA. She's a woman in a thousand. I knew that.

COLIN. She said to me, " You'd better go for Dr. Harvester."
(*With a sudden falter.*) By God, I shall never get the sound of her
voice out of my ears.

LICONDA (*rising*). Hold on, old man. (*Crossing to* COLIN.) It's
no good you going to pieces. Don't tell me any more if it upsets you.

COLIN (*pulling himself together*). No, I'm all right. There's
nothing more to tell. Mother said, " Nurse and I'll see to Stella."
That seemed to pull Nurse Wayland up. She came forward and
she and Mother began to get Stella round. I went into Maurice's
room. I felt his pulse and I put my hand on his heart. He looked
as if he was asleep. I knew he was dead. I got the car and went to
Dr. Harvester's and brought him back with me. (*Moving down* L.)
He said he thought poor Maurice had been dead for a good two
hours.

LICONDA. Did he say what had happened ?

COLIN (*turning, below the armchair* L. *of the table*). He thinks it
may have been an embolism. Or perhaps heart failure, you know.

LICONDA (*by the armchair* C.). How about Stella ?

COLIN. She's all right, thank God. She came to after a bit.
My God, she did give me a fright.

LICONDA. I don't wonder.

COLIN. Harvester wanted her to go to bed, but she wouldn't.
She's in Maurice's room now.

LICONDA. What about your mother ?

COLIN. Harvester's with her. He had to go and see some
patients, but he said he'd come back, and he turned up just before
you did. Here he is.

(*As he says these words,* DR. HARVESTER *enters up* R., *and comes
down* R.C. *He and* MAJOR LICONDA *shake hands.*)

HARVESTER. Hulloa, Major.

LICONDA. This is a very sad errand that has brought you here,
Doctor.

HARVESTER (*at* R.C.). It's naturally been a dreadful shock to
Mrs. Tabret and Stella.

(COLIN *goes to the desk* L., *for his letters.*)

LICONDA. How is Mrs. Tabret ?

HARVESTER (*to below the settee*). She's bearing up wonderfully.
She's very much upset, but she's trying not to show it. She has
a great deal of self-control.

LICONDA. I wonder if she'd like to see me.

HARVESTER. I'm sure she would.

COLIN (*turning at the desk*). Shall I run up and see ?

LICONDA (*moving to below the armchair* C.). It would be very
kind of you, Colin.

(COLIN *crosses to above the table.*)

Say that if she doesn't want to be bothered with me she has only to say so. I shall quite understand. I don't want to be a nuisance, but if it'll be any comfort to her to see me I shall be only too glad.

COLIN (*crossing up* R.). All right.

(*He exits.*)

LICONDA (*moving up* C. *to the french window* L.). You know, I've known Mrs. Tabret for over thirty years. Her husband was in the India Civil.

HARVESTER (*moving across to* L.C.). Yes, she told me.

LICONDA. They were almost the first people I got to know at all well when I went out to India. She's one of the best, you know. She always was. Everybody liked her.

HARVESTER (*sitting on the* L. *arm of the armchair* L.C.). Of course, I've seen a good deal of her during the last four years. She's really been wonderful. So has Stella, for the matter of that.

LICONDA (*moving down* R.C.). One can't help being rather thankful it's all over. (*He sits on the settee.*) But I could wish the end hadn't come quite so suddenly.

HARVESTER. Oh, why? It's much better that he should have passed out like that rather than get inflammation of the lungs or something of that sort that he just hadn't the strength to fight against.

LICONDA. So far as he was concerned, yes. I was thinking of his mother and Stella.

(NURSE WAYLAND *enters up* R. *She wears her nurse's uniform, and moves across to the table* L.C. HARVESTER *and* LICONDA *rise.*)

HARVESTER. Hulloa, Nurse. I thought you were having a rest.

LICONDA. Good morning.

NURSE. Good morning, Major. I'm glad you came round. Mrs. Tabret will be glad to see you.

HARVESTER. I told you to go and lie down, Nurse.

NURSE. I couldn't. I was too restless.

LICONDA. I'm afraid it's been as great a shock to Nurse Wayland as to the rest of us. After all, she'd been looking after Maurice for a long time.

NURSE. Yes, it's been a great shock to me. He was a dear. One couldn't help admiring him. He bore his terrible misfortune with so much courage.

HARVESTER. He was splendid.

NURSE. I naturally grew attached to him. He was always so gay and so grateful for what one did for him.

LICONDA (*turning down* R., *to the fireplace*). I suppose you'll try to get a good long holiday before you take another job.

NURSE. I haven't made any plans yet.

HARVESTER. To tell you the truth, you're looking all in.

NURSE (*listlessly*). Am I? (*She moves to above and* R. *of the chair* R. *of the table.*)

HARVESTER. You must try not to take it too hard.

NURSE.   A nurse naturally doesn't like to lose a patient. Especially so unexpectedly.

HARVESTER.   It was always on the cards that he'd go out suddenly.

NURSE (*moving slowly down a little*, R. *of the chair*). Like a candle that you blow out when you don't want it any more. Where does the flame go then ?

(DR. HARVESTER *looks at her for a moment reflectively, then takes a pace to below the table.*)

HARVESTER (*kindly*). My dear, I'm afraid you're taking poor Maurice's death a good deal more to heart than is quite wise.

NURSE (*with bitterness*). Did you think he was only a case to me ? Even a nurse is human. (*Crossing slowly to below the settee.*) Strange as it may seem, she has a heart like other people.

HARVESTER.   Of course she has a heart. (*Moving up*, R. *of the table.*) But it doesn't do her or her patients any good if she allows her emotions to get the better of her common sense. (*He is now up* C., *below the french windows.*)

NURSE.   Does that mean you think I've been inefficient ?

HARVESTER (*turning and moving down again*). No, of course not. Heaven knows, you never spared yourself. You take my advice, my dear, and go for a holiday. What you want is a real rest.

NURSE (*not looking at him*).   What is it, in your opinion, that Maurice Tabret actually died of ?

HARVESTER (*at* C.).   Heart failure.

NURSE.   Everybody dies of heart failure.

HARVESTER.   Of course. (*Moving* L.C., *below the table.*) But that's as good a thing as any to put on the death certificate.

NURSE.   Are you going to have a post-mortem ?

HARVESTER (*turning to her*).   No, why should I ? It's quite unnecessary.

NURSE (*looking him full in the face*).   I don't agree with you.

HARVESTER (*without a trace of asperity*).   I'm sorry. But it's my affair. If I'm prepared to sign the death certificate I don't know that anyone else has any right to say anything about it.

NURSE.   You've told me half a dozen times that Maurice Tabret might have lived for years.

HARVESTER.   So he might. I can tell you now that it's a blessing for everybody concerned with him that he didn't.

NURSE (*very deliberately*).   Dr. Harvester, Maurice Tabret was murdered.

(*A short pause.* LICONDA *is slightly startled.*)

HARVESTER.   What *are* you talking about ?

NURSE.   Do you want me to repeat it ? Maurice Tabret was murdered.

HARVESTER.   Rubbish.

LICONDA (*moving to the* R. *end of the settee*).   I daresay you're not quite yourself this morning, Nurse. It's very natural. But you must try to be reasonable. You oughtn't to say things that you can't possibly mean.

NURSE (*turning and facing* LICONDA). I'm in complete possession of my senses, Major Liconda, and I know perfectly well what I'm saying.

LICONDA. Do you mean to say that you intended that statement to be taken literally ?

NURSE. Quite.

LICONDA (*gravely*). It's a very serious one, you know.

NURSE. I'm aware of that.

HARVESTER (*taking a pace towards her*). It's grotesque.

NURSE (*moving to below the chair* R. *of the table*). You've known me for five years, Dr. Harvester. Have I ever given you to imagine that I'm a neurotic or hysterical woman, given to talking in a wild and exaggerated way ?

LICONDA (*moving in, and sitting on the settee*). Let us listen to what Nurse Wayland has to say. (*He motions to her, and she sits,* R. *of the table.*) Do you mean by any chance that you are dissatisfied with the way your patient was treated by Doctor Harvester ?

HARVESTER (*moving up* L. *of the table*). By George, that never occurred to me. (*Above the table.*) Is that it, Nurse ? Don't hesitate to say anything you want to. I shan't be in the least offended.

NURSE. So far as I could judge, you did everything for Maurice Tabret that medical skill could do.

LICONDA. Besides, he was surely seen by several specialists.

HARVESTER. Half a dozen at the least.

(*A very slight pause.*)

LICONDA. Well, Nurse Wayland ?

NURSE. I am a trained nurse, Major Liconda ; you can't imagine that if Maurice Tabret had died as the result of an error in treatment on Dr. Harvester's part I should be so heartless as to distress the relatives by mentioning it. I've made a definite charge and I stick to it.

HARVESTER. The charge being that some person or persons unknown murdered Maurice Tabret ?

NURSE. Yes.

HARVESTER (*to* L. *of the armchair*). But, my dear, why *should* anyone want to murder poor Maurice ?

NURSE. That at present is no business of mine.

HARVESTER (*taking a pace to below the armchair*). Now, look here, Nurse, you know just as well as I do that everyone connected with him was devoted to Maurice. No one was ever more surrounded with love and affection than he was. It's incredible that anyone should even have *wished* him harm.

NURSE. Whatever I may think or may not think I am at liberty to keep to myself. I am not in the witness box.

HARVESTER. The witness box ? (*Mockingly.*) Do you already see yourself giving sensational evidence at the Old Bailey ?

NURSE. I can honestly say that I can imagine nothing more hateful than the notoriety that would be forced upon me if I were obliged to appear in court.

HARVESTER. There'd be notoriety all right. This is the sort of thing that would be jam for the papers. Come, now, you know just as well as I do that Maurice died of natural causes. What on earth is the use of making a fuss and getting everyone upset ?

NURSE. If he died of natural causes a post-mortem will prove it and then I shall have nothing more to say.

HARVESTER (*irritably, moving away down* L.). I'm not going to have a post-mortem. You know how the relatives hate it.

NURSE. Are you afraid of what it will show ?

HARVESTER (*with decision, turning to her*). Of course not.

NURSE (*defiantly, rising*). I warn you that if you sign the death certificate I shall go straight to the coroner and make a protest.

HARVESTER. I should have thought the Tabrets had had enough to put up with, without being obliged to go through the ordeal you want to force upon them.

NURSE (*moving a little* R., *to* L. *of the settee*). Major Liconda, you were in the Indian Police, weren't you ? You ought to know about such things. Will you tell me what is the duty of a nurse who has reason to believe that her patient has come to his death by foul play ?

LICONDA. I suppose her duty is quite clear. But I think she should be very sure that her reasons are valid before she exposes to distress and publicity a family that has treated her with unvarying kindness.

HARVESTER. What are your reasons, anyway ? You've made a charge, but to the best of my recollection you haven't given us an inkling of what it's based on.

NURSE (*turning to face* HARVESTER). If you'd been willing to have a post-mortem nothing need have been said till we knew the results of it. (*Moving a little, to* C.) But you've put me with my back to the wall. Major Liconda is right. Everyone in this house has treated me with the greatest consideration. I do at least owe it to them to make no charges that may directly or indirectly concern them behind their backs.

HARVESTER. Does that mean you want them sent for ?

NURSE. Please. (*She moves to* R. *of the chair* R. *of the table.*)

LICONDA (*rising*). I think it's best. (*Moving down* R.) You've been so definite, Nurse Wayland, that neither Dr. Harvester nor I can keep the matter to ourselves. (*Turning at* R.) However distressing it may be I think Maurice's family should know what you have to say.

NURSE. I'm quite prepared to tell them. In point of fact, I think Mrs. Tabret is just coming.

LICONDA (*to below the settee*). Where is Stella ?

HARVESTER. Do you want her, too ?

LICONDA. I think it's better.

HARVESTER (*turning up. L. of the armchair*). I'll see if I can find her.

LICONDA. I believe she's in Maurice's room.

(HARVESTER *exits up* L.)

NURSE (*after a short pause*). Don't judge me till you've heard all I have to say, Major Liconda.

LICONDA (*with a certain severity, moving to up* R.C.). Miss Wayland, I happen to be a very old friend of the Tabrets and deeply attached to Mrs. Tabret. I regret that you should think it your duty at this moment of all others to add to their great sorrow. I can only hope that you will be shown *not* to have been justified.

NURSE. In that case you will have good reason to throw me out of the house, bag and baggage.

LICONDA. It is not my house, Miss Wayland, and I doubt whether Colin Tabret would be willing to depute that pleasant task to me.

NURSE. I'm just as glad to know who are my friends and who are my enemies. (*She turns up stage to the french windows.*)

(LICONDA *moves to above the table* L.C., *and turns as* MRS. TABRET *enters up* R. *with* COLIN. *She goes up to* MAJOR LICONDA *with a little smile. She is calm and composed.* COLIN *stands* L. *of the settee table.*)

MRS. TABRET. My dear old friend.

LICONDA (*meeting her at* C.). I felt that I must come and see you for a moment, my dear. I'm sure you know how deeply I sympathise with you, but I wanted to tell you that if in any way I can be of service to you . . .

MRS. TABRET (*interrupting him with a little smile*). It was very kind of you to come and just like you. (*She turns and moves to below the* R. *end of the settee.*)

LICONDA (*to* L. *of the settee*). I'm relieved to see that you're bearing so bravely what must have been a bitter blow.

(MRS. TABRET *sits.*)

MRS. TABRET. I am trying to put my own feelings away out of sight and mind. I want only to think that my son has ended his long martyrdom. I will not weep because he is dead. I will rejoice because he is free.

(STELLA *enters up* L., *followed by* DR. HARVESTER. *She is all in white.* HARVESTER *moves down* L.)

STELLA (*to* LICONDA—*moving to* C.). Dr. Harvester told me you were here and wanted to see me.

LICONDA. I wanted first of all to tell you how much I feel for you in your sad loss.

STELLA. You know, Maurice and I often talked of death. He was never afraid of it. He didn't attach very much importance to it. He told me that he didn't wish me to wear mourning for him. He wanted me to go about and do things exactly as if he were alive.

MRS. TABRET. He loved you so much, Stella. He put your happiness above everything.

STELLA. Yes. (*Crossing to the settee.*) You know, Maurice never quite believed that with this life everything ended for him. (*She sits* L. *of* MRS. TABRET.) He didn't believe in a great many things that many people still more or less believe in . . .

MRS. TABRET (*interrupting*). I could never bring myself to teach my children what I couldn't myself believe. When they were little and I used to sit in the evenings in our house and look at the multitudinous stars sweeping across the blue sky of India and thought of what we are, so transitory and so insignificant, and yet with such a capacity for suffering, such a passion for beauty, I was overwhelmed by the mystery and the immensity of the universe. I could not conceive what was the cause of all those worlds I saw above me, nor what was the power that guided them, but my heart was filled with amazement and awe. What I vaguely divined was too stupendous to fit into the limits of any creed of men.

(COLIN *moves quietly above the settee table to down* R., *at the fireplace.*)

STELLA. You know how Maurice was always laughing and joking. Even when he was speaking seriously he kept a little twinkle in his eye, so that you weren't quite sure he wasn't making fun of himself. I think he'd never quite grown out of some of those beliefs that I suppose he'd acquired unconsciously in his childhood from nurses and servants.

MRS. TABRET. We always had native ayahs. Heaven knows what they taught the children.

(LICONDA *moves quietly to above the table* L.C.)

STELLA. He didn't believe with his reason, but in some strange way with his nerves or his heart, that perhaps there was something in the eastern notion of the transmigration of souls.

(NURSE WAYLAND *moves away from the windows, coming a little down* C.)

(*Rising and moving to* NURSE WAYLAND.) I had something to say to you, Nurse. You'll be leaving us very soon now, I suppose?

NURSE. I suppose so.

STELLA. I want to thank you for everything you did for Maurice, and I want you to know how deeply grateful I am to you.

NURSE. I did no more than my duty.

STELLA (*with a charming smile*). Oh, no, you did much more than that. If it had been only your duty you could never have been so immensely thoughtful. You've been so awfully kind.

NURSE (*a trifle sullenly*). Your husband was a very easy patient. He was always anxious not to give trouble.

STELLA (*bringing* NURSE WAYLAND *down to below the chair* R. *of the table*). I've got a little plan that I want to tell you about. You've had a long and hard time here. And your month's holiday a year has been very little rest. You've often talked to me about your sister in South Africa and I know how much you've wanted to travel. If you'll allow me I should like to make it possible for you to go out there and have a good time.

NURSE (*stonily; on the defensive*). I don't think I understand what you mean.

STELLA (*a little shyly, but in a manner that is disarming*). Well, my dear, a nurse's salary is never very large. I know that Maurice has left me everything he had. It would be dear of you if you'd let me make you a present of a few hundred pounds, so that you could go for a nice long journey and need not think of earning your living for a while.

NURSE (*hoarsely, trembling in her effort to control herself*). Do you think I would take money from you ? Is that what you take me for ?

STELLA (*surprised, but not taking her very seriously*). But what on earth is the harm of it ? Come, Nurse, don't be unreasonable. You know I don't want to offend you.

NURSE. What I've done I've been paid for. If I wasn't satisfied with the payment I received I only had to go.

STELLA (*taken aback, as though she had been suddenly slapped in the face*). Nurse ! (*Retreating a pace.*) What *is* the matter ? Why do you speak to me like that ?

HARVESTER (*moving in, to below the armchair* L.C.). You mustn't take what Nurse Wayland says too literally. She really isn't herself to-day.

LICONDA (*above the table*). No, Harvester, it's no good taking up that attitude. The position is much too serious. Stella, I've got something very unpleasant to tell you. I would sooner not have added to your present trouble, but I'm afraid it can't be avoided.

STELLA. What is it ?

LICONDA. Nurse Wayland is not satisfied that Maurice died from heart failure.

STELLA. But if Dr. Harvester says so ? Surely he knows best.

HARVESTER. I am prepared to sign the death certificate. I have no doubt in my mind of the cause of death.

LICONDA. Nurse Wayland thinks there ought to be a post-mortem.

STELLA (*with the utmost determination*). Never. Never. (*She goes to below the settee and turns.*) Poor Maurice's body has suffered enough. I won't have him cut about to satisfy an idle curiosity. I absolutely refuse.

LICONDA. I understand that an autopsy cannot be held except with the consent of the next of kin.

NURSE. Or on the order of the coroner.

STELLA. What does she mean by that ?

LICONDA (*crossing to* C.). I'm afraid she means that if you persist in your refusal she will go to the proper authority and make the statement she has already made to Dr. Harvester and me.

STELLA. What is the statement ?

LICONDA (*turning to the* NURSE). Do you wish to repeat it, Nurse Wayland ?

NURSE (*very coolly, almost with insolence*). Not particularly. I have no objection to your doing so.

HARVESTER. Do you really insist on going through with this, Nurse ? What you said to the Major and me was more or less confidential, wasn't it ? Don't you think you'd better reflect a little more ? If anything further is said the matter must necessarily go out of our control. I think you should consider the consequences of your attitude and the harm that may arise.

NURSE. I can't keep silent. I should never forgive myself.

LICONDA (*to the others*). Nurse Wayland states that Maurice's death was not due to his illness, but to some other cause.

STELLA. I'm dreadfully sorry, but I don't understand. What other cause could have brought about his death ?

LICONDA. She says he was murdered.

(COLIN *and* STELLA *start.* COLIN *moves to* L. *of the settee table.*
MRS. TABRET *smothers a cry.*)

STELLA. Murdered ? (*She sits slowly on the settee.*) You must be mad, Nurse.

LICONDA. Harvester and I have pointed out to her that he was regarded by everyone connected with him with the greatest affection.

COLIN. It's preposterous.

STELLA. After the first shock I'm almost inclined to laugh. Really, Nurse, you must be very nervous and overwrought to have got such an idea in your head. Is that why you were so funny when I asked you to accept enough money to take a year's holiday ?

NURSE. I had no wish that the matter should go so far now. If Dr. Harvester had agreed to my suggestion of having a post-mortem nothing need have been said till it was discovered if my suspicions were justified or not.

HARVESTER (*turning away up* L. *of the armchair*). Willing to wound and yet afraid to strike, Nurse Wayland ? (*He turns, facing her.*)

NURSE (*turning on him*). You have forced me into this position, Dr. Harvester. I only did my duty in telling you my very grave suspicions, and the moment I did, you took up a definitely hostile attitude towards me.

HARVESTER. Well, if you want to know, I thought you silly, nervous, and hysterical. Good heavens, I've been in practice long enough to know how wildly people talk. I should be kept pretty busy if I paid any attention, for instance, to what one woman says about another.

NURSE. Or is it that you're frightened to death of a scandal ?

HARVESTER. I admit I shouldn't welcome publicity. But I can honestly say that if it were my duty I wouldn't let my own interests stop me from doing it. In this case I don't think it is my duty. I am quite satisfied that there is no reason why I shouldn't sign the necessary documents.

COLIN (*moving to* L. *of the settee*). All that is neither here nor there. Nurse Wayland has presumably some grounds for her statement. Perhaps she'd better give them.

LICONDA. Yes, she has. I thought it better she should speak before all concerned.

NURSE (*turning up a pace, to* L. *of* COLIN). It was my wish to do so. I don't want to do anything underhand.

STELLA. Go on, Nurse Wayland.

NURSE (*to* LICONDA). I daresay you know that Mr. Maurice often had bouts of sleeplessness. Dr. Harvester had prescribed various sedatives. But he found that chloralin was the one he supported best. (*To* HARVESTER.) Is that true ?

HARVESTER. Quite. I explained to Maurice the danger of his growing dependent on drugs and begged him not to take a dose without my permission or Nurse Wayland's.

NURSE. I'm quite sure that he never did.

HARVESTER. So am I. He was very sensible and he understood my point. He certainly wasn't lacking in self-control.

NURSE (*coming down a pace*). Will you tell Major Liconda what instructions you gave me last night ?

HARVESTER. He was excited and over-wrought. I asked Nurse Wayland to give him a tabloid and told him that if he woke in the night he could take it. I thought he'd probably drop off for half an hour or so and then wake up and not be able to get to sleep again.

NURSE. I dissolved a tabloid in half a glass of water and put it by his side. I noticed that there were only five tabloids left in the bottle and I made up my mind to order some more. This morning the bottle was empty.

STELLA (*puzzled*). That's very strange.

(*A pause.* NURSE *looks at* STELLA.)

NURSE. Very !

HARVESTER (*moving down a little*). How did you happen to notice ?

NURSE (*turning to* HARVESTER). I was tidying up. I thought it better to put away all the medicines and dressings and so on.

STELLA (*to* HARVESTER). Would five tabloids have a fatal effect ?

NURSE. Six. I left one dissolved in water by the side of his bed.

HARVESTER. Yes. (*He sits in the armchair* L. *of the table.*) There's little doubt that the effect would be fatal.

STELLA. It's incredible.

(COLIN *moves a pace nearer to* STELLA.)

It's surely much more likely that someone took them for his own use.

COLIN (*turning to the* NURSE). Are you absolutely sure that last night the bottle contained five tabloids?

NURSE. Absolutely. (*She turns away and moves to below the chair* R. *of the table.*) If anyone took them for his own use it must have been after I went to bed. (*She sits, slowly,* R. *of the table.*)

STELLA. But no one went into Maurice's room last night after that but me. I went in to say good night to him.

(*A slight pause.*)

LICONDA (*moving to* R.C.). How do you know that no one else went into his room?

STELLA. Who could have? There was only Colin and Mother.

LICONDA (*to* MRS. TABRET). You went upstairs as I was letting myself out, Millie.

MRS. TABRET. I was very tired. (*With the shadow of a smile.*) I didn't see any reason to wait while Colin and Stella and the Doctor ate a bacon sandwich.

LICONDA. You didn't go into Maurice's room last night, Colin?

COLIN. No, why should I? (*He sits on the* L. *arm of the settee.*) I don't want a sleeping-draught to make me sleep.

STELLA. You're not under the impression that I took the tabloids, I suppose, Nurse Wayland?

HARVESTER (*leaning forward a little*). If you had you could presumably produce at least four of them. Believe me, if you'd taken twenty-five grains of chloralin at midnight you wouldn't be sitting there now.

NURSE. The fact remains that five tabloids disappeared last night. Where are they?

HARVESTER (*sitting back a little*). There's always the possibility that they were taken maliciously by someone who wanted to make trouble.

NURSE (*sitting erect, her hands on the arms of her chair*). Do you mean me, Dr. Harvester? What do you think I can get out of making trouble? Really I don't know how such a stupid idea can have crossed your mind. Why should I have asked you to have a post-mortem if I knew for certain—as I must if I'd taken the tabloids out of sheer malice—that it would discover nothing?

(LICONDA *moves a pace* L., *and listens carefully.*)

COLIN. Isn't it possible that they could have been taken by somebody this morning?

LICONDA (*turning to look at* COLIN). Who?

COLIN. The housemaid, for instance.

(*The* NURSE *relaxes a little.*)

LICONDA. Chloralin is not a very common drug. I shouldn't

have thought a housemaid would ever have heard of it. It's not as though it were aspirin.

HARVESTER. I don't know about that. There have been cases in the papers. It's not safe to take it for granted that a housemaid wouldn't have got into the habit of taking something when she couldn't sleep.

STELLA. Well, it's very easy to make sure. (*Rising.*) It's Alice who did Maurice's room. (*Crossing down* R.) Let us send for her. (*She is about to press the bell push.*)

NURSE. That is unnecessary. She was frightened at the idea of going in. I told her she need not and said I would clean up the room and put everything to rights myself. I'm quite sure she has not been in this morning.

STELLA (*moving up* R.). What are we to do, Mother ? (*She moves to above the settee table.*)

MRS. TABRET. You must do exactly what you think fit.

LICONDA (*moving to above the table* L.C., *and addressing* HARVESTER). Doctor, is it possible that Maurice can have died from chloral poisoning ?

HARVESTER (*with a slightly impatient movement*). I have told you that I am satisfied that death was due to natural causes.

LICONDA. I wasn't asking that.

HARVESTER. Yes, of course, it's possible. But I don't for an instant believe it.

(STELLA *moves above* COLIN *and then down on his* L.)

NURSE (*turning in her chair, to* MRS. TABRET). I know that this must add awfully to your grief, Mrs. Tabret. I can't tell you how sorry I am. It seems dreadful that I should have to repay all your kindness to me by increasing your troubles.

MRS. TABRET. My dear, I'm quite ready to believe that you will do nothing and say nothing but what you think is right.

STELLA (*coming down a little*). I'm all confused. It's come as such a dreadful shock. (*To the* NURSE, *with a pace towards her.*) Do you *really* think that Maurice died of an overdose of his sleeping-draught ?

NURSE (*very deliberately, looking her straight in the eyes*). I do.

STELLA. It's awful.

NURSE (*still looking at* STELLA). I think I should tell you that when I found the tabloids were missing I looked in the glass in which I'd dissolved the one I'd prepared for him. There was still about a dessertspoonful of liquid in the bottom of it. I have put it aside and I suggest that it should be analysed.

MRS. TABRET (*with faint mockery*). You are wasted on your profession, Nurse Wayland. You have all the makings of a detective.

LICONDA (*moving down,* L. *of* HARVESTER). But wouldn't a draught in which half a dozen tabloids had been dissolved be very unpalatable ?

HARVESTER.   It would be rather bitter. I suppose if one swallowed it down at a gulp one would hardly notice till one had already drunk it.

(LICONDA *sits, down* L.)

STELLA.   It all sounds very circumstantial. I'm afraid there's a dreadful probability in Nurse Wayland's story.

COLIN (*standing*). But, my dear, it's absurd. Who on earth would have thought of murdering Maurice ? It's out of the question.

STELLA.   Oh, that, yes. I wasn't thinking of that. Nurse Wayland can't seriously think that anyone deliberately gave Maurice an overdose of his sleeping-draught.   But I'm beginning to be desperately afraid that perhaps he took it himself.

HARVESTER.   Suicide ?

STELLA (*with distress*). He wasn't himself last night. He was very strange. I'd never seen him so nervous.

LICONDA (*rising*). Was there any reason for that ?

STELLA (*after a moment's hesitation*). I'm afraid so. You see — I'd been to *Tristan*. And we'd seen it together . . . the night we got engaged. (*In a low voice.*) It upset him to think of the past.

LICONDA (*moving a little in, and up stage*). Did he speak of suicide ?

STELLA.   No.

LICONDA.   Had he ever done so ?

STELLA.   Never. I don't believe it had entered his head.

LICONDA (L. *of the armchair* L.C.). What made you think he was upset last night ?

STELLA (*much moved*). He did a thing he'd never done before. It was dreadfully painful. He cried. He cried in my arms.

NURSE.   Why ?

STELLA (*desperately*). Really, Nurse Wayland, there are some things I can't tell you. What passed between my husband and myself was between ourselves. It concerned nobody but us.

NURSE.   I beg your pardon. I should have thought it better for your own sake to be frank.

STELLA.   What do you mean ? Are you accusing me of holding anything back ?

NURSE.   I'm not accusing anybody.

LICONDA (*crossing slowly towards* STELLA). My dear, I won't ask you anything that is painful for you to answer. But there's just this. If there's anything in what Miss Wayland says I suppose there'll have to be an inquest. The coroner will certainly ask you if your husband said anything at all that might indicate that suicide was in his mind.

STELLA (*with a deep sigh*). He said it would have been better if the accident had killed him outright. But he wasn't thinking of himself, he was thinking of me.

LICONDA.   That's very important.   (*He turns and moves to above the table* L.C.)

STELLA.   Oh, Nurse, don't be hard on us. Don't be vindictive because I've been rather sharp with you. My nerves are all on edge to-day. After all, it's rather natural, isn't it ? If poor Maurice did take an overdose of something, can't you square it with your conscience to say nothing about it ? He had so little to live for. Can't you spare us the distress and horror of a post-mortem and an inquest ?

(COLIN *puts an arm round* STELLA *and leads her to the settee. She sits.*)

LICONDA. The question is if Dr. Harvester is still willing to sign the death certificate ? (*He looks at* HARVESTER.)

HARVESTER (*rising*). I think Nurse Wayland may very well have been mistaken about the tabloids. I can see no reason why I shouldn't. (*He turns up* L. *of the armchair.*)

NURSE (*deliberately; rising*). But you see, I am quite convinced that Maurice Tabret did not commit suicide.

LICONDA. For what reason ?

NURSE (*turning up*, R. *of her chair, and facing* LICONDA). Well, here's one of them. There was a little liquid still in the glass from which he drank. About a dessertspoonful. You remember I mentioned that, and I put the glass away so that the liquid could be examined.

LICONDA. Yes.

NURSE. Surely if a man were going to commit suicide he would drink the entire contents of the glass either in one gulp or two. He wouldn't risk making a bad job of what he was about by leaving something at the bottom. Least of all a man like Maurice Tabret.

COLIN (*by the* L. *end of the settee, his hand over* STELLA'S, *on the settee arm*). That seems very far-fetched to me.

LICONDA. I must say it seems rather a small point.

COLIN. Besides, the stuff hasn't been analysed yet.

LICONDA. Is your conviction based on nothing more than that, Nurse Wayland ?

NURSE. No, it is not. Although Mr. Tabret was very good and I didn't believe he would ever take a tabloid without leave, one knows that it's very easy to get into the habit of drug-taking and then you can't be certain about anyone. Isn't that so, Dr. Harvester ?

HARVESTER. Yes, I suppose it is.

NURSE. Sometimes he was terribly depressed. I didn't think it wise to let him have within reach the power of putting an end to himself.

STELLA. I never saw him depressed.

NURSE (*bitterly; looking at* STELLA). I know you didn't. You never saw anything.

STELLA (*sitting erect*). Nurse Wayland, what have I done to you ? (*She rises.*) Why do you talk to me like that ? (*Crossing to* R. *of* NURSE.) Your face is all twisted with hate of me. I don't understand.

NURSE. Don't you ?

(*The two women stare at one another for a moment, then* STELLA
gives a little shudder and turns her head away.)

STELLA. I'm beginning to be frightened of you. What sort of
a woman are you that we've had in this house for three years ?

MRS. TABRET (*in a soothing tone*). There's nothing to be frightened
of, darling. Don't give way to your nerves.

NURSE (*to* STELLA). Because he joked and laughed when you
were there, did it never occur to you that there were moments
when he was overwhelmed with black misery ?

STELLA (*with deep sympathy*). Poor lamb, why did he insist on
hiding it from me ?

NURSE (*with a sort of restrained violence*). His one aim was to
make his suffering easy for *you* to bear. Whatever pain he had, he
hid from you so that you shouldn't have the distress of being sorry
for him.

STELLA. It's dreadful that you should say such things. You
make me feel that I was so cruel to him.

NURSE (*with increasing bitterness*). Everything had to be hidden
from you. When you were coming the medicine bottles and the
dressings had to be put away, so that there should be nothing to
remind you that there was anything the matter with him.

STELLA. I would willingly have done everything for him that
you did. It was his most earnest wish that I shouldn't concern
myself with the horrid part of his illness.

MRS. TABRET. That is true, Nurse. I'm sorry you don't think
that Stella did all she could for Maurice. As his mother I'm perhaps
no less competent to judge than you. I have only admiration for
her unselfishness and devotion.

STELLA. Oh, Mother. (*She crosses to below the settee.*)

MRS. TABRET (*touching* STELLA'S *hand, with sympathy*). I always
think we do best by people when we help them in the way they
want to be helped rather than in the way we may think they should
be helped.

LICONDA. There's something in that, Nurse Wayland.

MRS. TABRET. I'm sure that Stella did Maurice most good by
answering him back in the same strain when he chaffed her and
when he laughed, laughing with him.

NURSE (*above and* R. *of the chair* R. *of the table*). I was nothing.
I was only his paid nurse. He didn't try to hide from me the despair
that filled his heart. He didn't have to pretend with me. He didn't
have to be good-tempered or amusing with me. He could be
morose and he knew I wouldn't mind. He could quarrel with me
and then say he was sorry if he'd hurt me and know he couldn't
hurt me.

STELLA (*turning slowly, the truth dawning on her that the* NURSE
had loved him). What are you telling us, Nurse Wayland ?

NURSE. I'm telling the truth at last.

STELLA (*sitting, slowly,* L. *of* MRS. TABRET). I wonder if you know
what strange truth it is.

LICONDA (*taking one pace towards* C.). But, Nurse, what you've been saying suggests that he did have at least moments of despair when he must have thought of suicide. We know that he was over-wrought last night. If his death was not due to natural causes, surely it's extremely likely that he brought it about himself.

NURSE (*looking at* LICONDA). It was just one of those moments that I was on my guard against. The chloralin was kept in the bathroom on an upper shelf that he could not possibly have got at. I had to stand on a chair myself to reach it.

LICONDA. If a man is determined to do a thing he can often surmount difficulties that others would have though insuperable.

NURSE (*coming down a pace*). Ask Dr. Harvester if it would have been possible for Maurice Tabret to cross the room and go into the bathroom and stand up on a chair.

(*The others look* L. *at* HARVESTER.)

HARVESTER. He had absolutely no power in the lower part of his body. His back was broken by the accident and the spinal cord terribly injured.

LICONDA (*taking a pace* L.). Couldn't he have crawled into the bathroom ?

HARVESTER. With a great deal of difficulty. Yes, I think he might have done that.

NURSE (*taking one pace towards her chair*). Could he have stood up on a chair ?

HARVESTER. No, I'm bound to admit that is absolutely out of the question.

LICONDA (*close to the table* L.C., *above it*). If he'd got into the bathroom, couldn't he have fished down the bottle with a stick or something ?

HARVESTER. Perhaps.

NURSE. Why do you say that, Dr. Harvester ? You know that he couldn't sit upright without help.

HARVESTER (*with a restless movement* L.). I'm not so anxious to put the worst construction on everything as you seem to be, Nurse Wayland.

NURSE. And if he'd got the bottle down, how could he have put it up in its place again ?

HARVESTER (*irritably*). After all, we don't know yet that Maurice died of an overdose of chloralin.

LICONDA. The matter can't be left like this, Harvester. I'm afraid there'll have to be an inquest.

HARVESTER (*moving to below the armchair* L.C.). Yes, obviously, I can't sign the death certificate now. I shall have to communicate with the coroner.

NURSE. I'm sorry, Dr. Harvester.

HARVESTER. I'm sure you are. (*Crossing to below the chair* R. *of the table.*) I suppose you think it's very self-seeking of me not to want to be mixed up in a scandal . . .

LICONDA (*cutting in, and moving down* L. *of the table*). Oh, come now, it's not going to be as bad as that. However distressing an inquiry may be to Maurice's family, I don't see how it can affect his doctor. For a hopeless invalid to take an overdose of his sleeping-draught is not so uncommon as to excite much comment.

HARVESTER. I suppose not. (*He sits,* R. *of the table.*)

(NURSE WAYLAND *withdraws a pace* R. *of the chair.*)

LICONDA. Many of us can only admire a man who has a fatal illness and prefers to end his life painlessly rather than endure useless suffering. He is more merciful to himself and to those he loves.

NURSE. Dr. Harvester knows as well as I do that if Maurice Tabret died of an overdose of chloralin he couldn't have taken it himself. There's only one word for it and you all know it. It was murder.

HARVESTER (*strongly, sitting erect*). That's why I'm absolutely convinced that he died of natural causes. I can't offer an explanation of the disappearance of those damned tabloids, but there must be an explanation.

COLIN (*moving down* R., *below the settee*). The most likely one is that Nurse Wayland was mistaken. (*Turning at the fireplace and moving in.*) Surely, if anyone had taken out half a dozen tabloids he would have put others in their place, aspirin or chlorate of potash or something, so that they wouldn't be missed. (*He finishes speaking, at the lower end of the settee.*)

NURSE. People don't think of everything. It's only because a murderer makes some mistake that he's caught.

HARVESTER (*springing to his feet*). But, damn it all, no one commits a murder without a motive. (*Turning up* R. *of his chair.*) No one had the smallest reason to wish Maurice dead. (*Breaking to up* L.C.)

NURSE. How do you know?

HARVESTER (*turning and coming down above the table* L.C.). Good God, how do I know that two and two are four? I know that everybody was devoted to him. And with reason, damn it. He was the best fellow in the world.

NURSE (*moving towards* HARVESTER). Did you know that his wife was going to have a baby?

STELLA (*with a gasp*). You fiend!

COLIN (*aghast*). Stella!

NURSE (*above and slightly* R. *of the chair by the table*). I suspected it last night when she nearly fainted. This morning I knew for certain.

STELLA (*rising*). What do you mean? (*Taking a pace up stage.*) Are you accusing me of having murdered my husband?

LICONDA (*very gravely, moving in a pace*). Is it true what she says, Stella?

(*There is a pause.* STELLA *does not speak. She sits slowly on the settee again. There is anguish in her eyes.* ALICE, *the parlourmaid, comes briskly in, up* R., *breaking the tension with the affairs of every day.*)

ALICE (*to up* R.C.). Shall I keep lunch back, madam ?
MRS. TABRET. Is it one o'clock ? No, you can serve up.
COLIN. We can't have lunch now, Mother.
MRS. TABRET. Why not ? Lay for two extra. Major Liconda and Dr. Harvester will be lunching.
ALICE. Very good, madam.

(*She exits.*)

(NURSE WAYLAND *moves up towards the windows.*)

COLIN. Mother, it's impossible. How can we all sit down together as though nothing had happened ?
MRS. TABRET (*looking up at* COLIN). I think it's just as well. We have a great deal more to say to one another. It will do none of us any harm to talk of other things for half an hour.
STELLA. I couldn't, I couldn't. Let me stay here.
MRS. TABRET (*firmly, her hand on* STELLA'S *knee*). I insist on your coming, my dear.
HARVESTER (*crossing to* R.C.). I must bolt round to my house, Mrs. Tabret. I'll have a bite there and come back immediately afterwards.
MRS. TABRET. Very well.

(HARVESTER *exits up* R.)

LICONDA (*moving in to below the chair* R. *of the table*). My dear, I couldn't think of imposing myself on you.
MRS. TABRET (*with a grim smile*). You must eat. Will you come, Nurse Wayland ?
NURSE (*up* C.). No.
MRS. TABRET. I'll have something sent up to your room.
NURSE. I want nothing.
MRS. TABRET. You may when it comes.

(ALICE *comes in again.*)

ALICE (*to up* R.C.). Lunch is served, madam.
MRS. TABRET (*giving* STELLA *her hand*). Come, Stella.

(*They rise. There is a general move towards up* R. *as the curtain falls.*)

CURTAIN.

ACT III

SCENE.—The same. Half an hour has passed.

STELLA *is standing at the french windows, looking into the garden off.*
COLIN *enters up* R. *from the hall.*

COLIN. Stella.

(STELLA *turns.*)

STELLA. Have you finished already ?

COLIN. More or less. (*Moving down* R.C.) I told Mother I
wanted to see if you were all right.

STELLA. Yes, I'm all right.

COLIN (*below the settee*). It was awful sitting there as though
nothing had happened. I don't know what induced Mother to make
us go through that farce.

STELLA (*with a shrug, turning down* C.). I daresay it was very
sensible. With the servants there it was obvious that we had to hold
our tongues. It gave us all a chance to collect ourselves.

COLIN (*moving up to* R. *of* STELLA). Stella, is it true ?

STELLA. Is what true ?

COLIN. What that woman said.

STELLA. About the baby ? I suppose so. (*Crossing him to
down* R.) Yes, it's true.

COLIN. Oh, Stella.

STELLA (*turning*). I wasn't sure. (*Moving slowly up to below the
settee.*) I was afraid. I thought it might be a false alarm. It's only
quite lately that I've been certain.

COLIN (*taking a pace towards her*). Why didn't you tell me ?

STELLA. I didn't want to.

COLIN. Not at all ? Were you going to let me go away without
knowing ?

STELLA. I didn't want to spoil those last weeks for you. Because
I worried there didn't seem to be any reason why you should be
worried, too.

COLIN (*moving nearer*). But what were you going to do ?

STELLA. I don't know. I was looking for some way out. (*Not
looking at him.*) I thought it would be easier when you were gone.
Whatever happened, I tnought I'd like to keep you out of it.

COLIN. Why ?

STELLA. I don't know . . . (*turning to look at him*) . . . unless
because I love you.

(*He takes her hands.*)

COLIN. Aren't I there to share your troubles with you ?

STELLA. I suppose women are very silly, when they tell a man that they're going to have a child by him. It seems rather important to them. They want to be made a fuss of. I couldn't expect you to feel joy or pride . . . only consternation.

COLIN. Oh, my dear, don't you know how devotedly I love you?

STELLA (*taking her hands away—easing down* R.). No, don't. Don't say anything that's going to upset me. I don't want to get emotional. (*She sits on the settee.*) If we've got to talk it over we'd better try to talk it over as calmly as we can.

COLIN (*moving nearer to her*). What is that dreadful woman going to say now?

STELLA. I don't know. I don't care . . . I don't know why I say that. I'm frightened to death. (*She pauses, looks up at* COLIN, *then rises.*) Oh, Colin, whatever happens you'll stand by me, won't you?

COLIN. Yes, I swear it.

(DR. HARVESTER *enters up* C., *from the garden.*)

HARVESTER (*moving down*). Oh, have you finished your luncheon already?

STELLA (*forcing a smile to her lips*). I'm afraid I couldn't make much of a pretence at eating. I wanted to be alone for a minute and came in here.

COLIN. I think Mother and Major Liconda will be here directly. They were just starting coffee when I left them.

HARVESTER. Where's Nurse Wayland? I came back rather soon because I thought I'd like to have a chat with her alone.

STELLA (*moving across* L.). Colin will go and fetch her. I suppose she lunched in her room.

COLIN. Right-ho.

(*He exits up* R.)

HARVESTER. I say, my dear, I hope this is going to come out all right.

STELLA (*turning at down* L.C.). It doesn't look much like it, does it?

HARVESTER. My word, you're taking this coolly.

STELLA (*below the table* L.C.). When the earth is opening under your feet and the heavens are falling it doesn't seem much use to run about like a frightened hen.

HARVESTER (*to beside the chair* R. *of the table*). Do you mind my giving you a bit of advice?

STELLA (*with a shade of irony*). I'd welcome it, but I think it's very unlikely I shall take it.

HARVESTER. Well, it's just this, if I were you I'd take very great care not to say anything to put up Nurse Wayland's back.

STELLA. She can't very well make things much more disagreeable than she has already.

HARVESTER. I'm not so sure of that. That's why I wanted to see her alone. You know she's not a bad sort, really. Now that she's had half an hour to calm down, I don't see why she shouldn't be more reasonable.

STELLA (*crossing towards the settee*). I wouldn't count on it in your place.

HARVESTER. I don't myself see what she has to get out of making a fuss.

STELLA (*turning, below the settee*). She's a very conscientious woman and she mistakes her hatred of me for the call of duty.

HARVESTER. The good are difficult to get on with, aren't they ?

STELLA (*smiling*). Fortunately they're so few, it's not often they seriously inconvenience the rest of us.

HARVESTER. She's got her knife into you all right.

STELLA (*moving a little towards him*). Dr. Harvester, will you tell me something ?

HARVESTER. If I can.

STELLA. Do you think it possible that Maurice could have guessed—about—the child ?

HARVESTER. I shouldn't think so.

STELLA (*after a moment, turning away* R). I'm so thankful. (*Sitting on the settee, facing down* R.) I couldn't have borne the thought that he died rather than expose me to shame and disgrace. He was capable of it, you know.

HARVESTER. I'm afraid that if Maurice died of an overdose of chloral he can't have taken it himself.

STELLA (*turning to look at* HARVESTER). But who could have given it him ?

HARVESTER. That is the question, isn't it ?

STELLA. Why couldn't that wretched woman leave me for a moment alone with my sorrow. You never knew Maurice in the old days. He was such a gallant figure. When I was in his room just now, I wept for myself as well as him. I wept for all the love I'd borne him in years gone by.

HARVESTER (*gently and sincerely*). I know . . . I know. (*He turns down* L.C.) However often your trade brings you in contact with death, you are overcome with the same dismay. (*Turning.*) It's so desperately final.

STELLA. I can't believe that it's final. It would be too unfair.

HARVESTER. There are some who think that if you only believe enough that a thing is true, it becomes true. Who am I to decide such matters ?

(*The door up* R. *is opened and* COLIN *comes in, immediately followed by the* NURSE.)

COLIN. Here is Nurse Wayland.

(*The* NURSE *comes down* R.C.)

STELLA (*rising; quietly*). Oh, Nurse, Dr. Harvester wishes to speak to you by himself. Colin and I will go into the garden.

NURSE. It's very kind of you. But I have nothing private to say to Dr. Harvester and I do not wish to listen to anything Dr. Harvester has to say that anyone else may not hear. I want to do nothing underhand.

HARVESTER (*turning away to* L.). I'm not going to ask you to do anything underhand.

NURSE (*moving to below the table* L.C.). I know exactly what you want to say to me. You're going to point out that everyone here has been very kind to me and very generous. And they're prepared to be still kinder and still more generous. And if I make a scandal I shall be exposed to every sort of unpleasantness and very likely have great difficulty in getting another job. On the other hand, if I hold my tongue I can go to South Africa and have a good time. Well, I won't.

STELLA (*coolly*). That seems very definite.

HARVESTER (*down* L.). All the same, I don't see how it can hurt you to listen to me for five minutes.

STELLA. Now I put my foot down. I'm not prepared to allow an appeal on my behalf to be made to Nurse Wayland.

COLIN (*up* R.C.). I think I hear my mother and the major.

HARVESTER. Then it's too late.

(STELLA *sits.* COLIN *goes up to the door* R., *and opens it for them.* MRS. TABRET *and* MAJOR LICONDA *enter.*)

MRS. TABRET (*moving down* R.C.). Have we kept you waiting? I hope you had everything you wanted in your room, Nurse?

NURSE (*down* L.C.). Everything, thank you, Mrs. Tabret.

MRS. TABRET. Won't you sit down? There's no use in your tiring yourself.

NURSE (*sitting* R. *of the table*). Thank you.

MRS. TABRET (*crossing down, below the settee*). Have you been talking things over?

HARVESTER. I've only just come, Mrs. Tabret.

(COLIN *moves down* R.)

MRS. TABRET (*sitting* L. *of* STELLA). I suppose we are in Nurse Wayland's hands. What have you decided to do, Nurse Wayland?

NURSE. I must do what I think is my duty, Mrs. Tabret.

MRS. TABRET. Of course. We should all do our duty, and how difficult it would be if at the same time we did not often make ourselves a trifle disagreeable to others.

NURSE. Mrs. Tabret, Major Liconda asked your daughter-in-law a question just before luncheon. She didn't answer it.

LICONDA (*who is at* R.C., *to* STELLA). I am afraid you must have thought me very impertinent. Nurse Wayland said that you were going to have a baby, and I asked you if it was true.

STELLA. It's quite true.

LICONDA (*struggling with his embarrassment*). I'm in a very false position. I am conscious that I am interfering in matters that are no affair of mine.

STELLA. My dear Major, I know that you are kindness itself. You've known Mrs. Tabret for ages and Maurice and Colin when they were small boys.

LICONDA. All the same you must see how difficult it is for me to ask the question that inevitably rises in one's mind.

STELLA. I'll answer without your asking. Of course it's quite impossible that Maurice should have been the father of the child I'm going to have. Since his accident he has been my husband only in name.

COLIN (*going to her, R. of the settee, and putting his hand round her shoulders*). I am the father, Major Liconda.

NURSE (*astounded*). You ?

(LICONDA *moves to above the table*.)

MRS. TABRET (*ironically*). Do you mean to say that it escaped your sharp eyes, Nurse, that Colin and Stella were in love with one another ?

STELLA (*with a little frightened gasp*). Did *you* know ?

MRS. TABRET. I think nowadays the young are apt to think their elders even more stupid than advancing years generally make them.

STELLA. Oh, Mother, what must you think of me ?

MRS. TABRET (*dryly*). Do you very much care ?

(LICONDA *moves quietly L., and a little downstage*.)

STELLA. I suppose I ought to be terribly ashamed of myself, but I must be sincere. I can no more help loving Colin than I can help the rain falling.

NURSE. You're shameless.

STELLA (*to* MRS. TABRET). But *you* have every right to think that I treated Maurice abominably. He's beyond the reach of pain, but I bitterly regret the pain I've caused you. I have no excuses to make for myself.

MRS. TABRET. My dear, don't you remember what I said to you last night ? I thanked you for all you had done for Maurice. Did you think I was talking at random ? I knew then that you were going to have a baby and that Colin was its father.

COLIN. Mother, I blame myself so awfully.

STELLA. You mustn't do that, darling. (*To* MRS. TABRET.) If a woman doesn't want a man to make love to her she can very easily prevent it. I didn't prevent Colin from making love to me because I wanted him to make love to me. I made him love me.

COLIN. Oh, Stella, how could I help loving you ? I don't blame myself for that. I blame myself because when I knew I loved you I didn't go away again. I felt that I'd loved her always, and that her love was home to me.

STELLA. Whatever you may think of me, Mother, and however badly you think I've behaved, I ask you to believe that I didn't give myself to Colin to gratify any passing whim. I loved him with all my heart.

MRS. TABRET. My dear, I know. You say you made him love you. Why do you say that except that you love him so much ?

STELLA. You mustn't think I didn't struggle against it. I said to myself that the only return I could make Maurice for all the devotion he gave me was by remaining faithful to him and loyal.

MRS. TABRET. I'm sure you did.

STELLA. I told myself that Maurice was a cripple, bedridden, sick, the victim of an unforeseen misfortune, and that it would be foul of me to betray him. I tried to drive Colin away. I did everything except ask him to go. I couldn't do that. I couldn't. I pretended to myself that it was on your account and on Maurice's. You hadn't seen him for so long. Maurice was so pleased to have him here.

MRS. TABRET. It's quite true that I hadn't seen Colin for a long time, and Maurice was tremendously pleased to have him here.

NURSE (rising; with exasperation). I don't understand you, Mrs. Tabret. You seem to be going out of your way to find excuses for your daughter-in-law. (Turning up, L. of her chair to above the table.) If you knew what was going on, why didn't you stop it ?

MRS. TABRET. I'm afraid I shall shock you, Miss Wayland ; I want to put it as delicately as I can, but it's a matter that we English have made indelicate by prudishness and hypocrisy. Stella is young, healthy and normal. Why should I imagine she has not got the instincts that I had at her age ?

(NURSE WAYLAND turns her head away with a little shiver of disgust.)

(Rising and crossing up to R. of NURSE.) When Maurice's accident made it impossible for him and Stella ever to live again as man and wife I asked myself if she would be able to support so false a relationship. Their love was deep and passionate, but it was rooted in sex. It might have come about with time that it would have acquired a more spiritual character. They did not have the time.

(The NURSE turns to look at MRS. TABRET for a moment. Then MRS. TABRET moves up towards the windows.)

NURSE (to STELLA, with irony, moving a pace down and towards the settee). May I ask how long you'd been married ?

STELLA. I was married to Maurice about a year before he crashed.

NURSE. A year. A whole year. (She turns away.)

MRS. TABRET (moving down L.C., addressing the NURSE). Out of his suffering a new love did spring up in Maurice's heart, a hungry, clinging, dependent love. I didn't know how long Stella would be content with that.

NURSE (*bitterly; turning from* MRS. TABRET). No one could say that you had much trust in human nature.

MRS. TABRET. I have a great deal. (*She sits.*) As much, in fact, as experience has taught me is justified. I knew that Stella's pity was infinite. I knew it was so great that she mistook it for love, and I prayed that she would never find out her mistake. She meant everything in the world to Maurice. Everything. But I feared the time would come when she could no longer stand the miserable life that was all he had to offer her. If she wanted to go I felt we hadn't the right to prevent her, and I knew that if she went Maurice would die.

STELLA. I would never have left him. It never entered my head that it was possible.

MRS. TABRET. I saw the strain that it began to be on her nerves. She was as kind as ever, and as gentle, but it was an effort, and what is the good you do worth unless you do it naturally as the flowers give their scent ?

NURSE (*moving to below the chair* R. *of the table*). I have never been given to understand that good is only good if it's easy to do.

MRS. TABRET. I don't suppose it is, but if it's difficult then I think it benefits the person who does it rather than the person it's done to. That is why it is more blessed to give than to receive.

NURSE. I don't understand you. (*She sits, slowly.*) I think what you say is odious and cynical.

MRS. TABRET. Then I'm afraid you'll think what I'm going to say now even more cynical and odious. I found myself half wishing that Stella should take a lover.

NURSE (*with horror*). Mrs. Tabret !

MRS. TABRET (*rising*). I was willing to shut my eyes to anything so long as she stayed with Maurice. I wanted her to be kind and thoughtful and affectionate to him, and I didn't care for the rest. (*She turns up,* L. *of her chair.*)

NURSE (*brokenly*). I had such a deep respect for you, Mrs. Tabret. I admired you so much. I used to think that when I was your age I'd like to be a woman like you.

MRS. TABRET (*up* L.C.; *turning*). When Colin came back and after a while I realised that he and Stella were in love with one another, I did nothing to prevent the almost inevitable consequences. I didn't deliberately say it to myself in so many words, that would have shocked me, but in my heart was a feeling that this would make it all right for Maurice. She wouldn't go now. She was bound to this house by a stronger tie than pity or kindness.

LICONDA (*moving in a pace*). Didn't it strike you what great dangers you were exposing them to ?

MRS. TABRET (*to* LICONDA). I didn't care. I only thought of Maurice. (*Turning and moving to* R.C.) When they were children I think I loved them equally. But since his accident I haven't had room in my heart for anyone but Maurice. (*Turning to face* LICONDA.) He was everything to me. For him I was prepared to sacrifice

Colin and Stella. (*Moving* R., *with a little gesture of appeal to* STELLA.) I hope they'll forgive me.

STELLA. Oh, my dear, as though there was anything to forgive.

NURSE (*rising*). You'll only laugh at me if I say I'm shocked. I can't help it. I'm shocked to the very depths of my soul.

MRS. TABRET (*below the* L. *end of the settee*). I was afraid you would be.

NURSE. I would have gone to the stake for my belief that no unclean thought had ever entered your head. Didn't it revolt you to think that your son's wife was having an affair with a man under your own roof?

MRS. TABRET (*sitting at the* L. *end of the settee*). I suppose I'm not very easily revolted. I've lived too long to think that my own standard of right and wrong is the only one possible. But I wonder why people don't see that morality isn't the same for everyone at the same time in the same country. There's a morality for the young, and a morality for the old. Perhaps we should all look upon these matters differently if our moral rules hadn't been made by persons who had forgotten the passion and the high spirits of youth. (*She looks directly at* NURSE WAYLAND.) Do you think it so very wicked if the young things surrender to the instincts that nature planted in them?

NURSE (*turning up,* R. *of her chair*). Did the probable result never occur to you?

MRS.. TABRET. A baby? It persuades me of Stella's essential innocence. Otherwise, she would have known how to avoid such an accident.

NURSE (*sardonically*). You must admit at all events that Maurice's death has come in the very nick of time to get her out of a very awkward predicament.

STELLA. Nurse, what a cruel—what a heartless thing to say.

LICONDA (*sternly; moving in, to below the armchair*). You must be very careful, Nurse. That sounds extremely like an accusation.

NURSE (*to* LICONDA). I wanted to accuse nobody. Do me the justice to admit that I started by saying that I was not satisfied with the circumstances and thought there should be a post-mortem. That was my right and my duty. Isn't that so, Dr. Harvester?

HARVESTER. I suppose it is.

NURSE. You've forced me to this. You asked me who could have a motive for murdering Maurice Tabret. In self-defence I was obliged to tell you that his wife was going to have a child of which he couldn't be the father.

(STELLA *rises.*)

STELLA. You talk of your duty, Nurse. (*She crosses up to* R. *of the* NURSE.) Are you sure that your motive for all this is anything more than your bitter hatred of me?

NURSE (*scornfully*). Why should I hate you? Believe me, I only despise you.

STELLA.   You hate me because you were in love with Maurice.

NURSE (*violently; retreating a pace*). I ? How dare you say that ?

STELLA (*coolly*). You gave it away. It had often seemed to me that you were fonder of Maurice than a nurse generally is of her patient and I used to chaff him about it. It never struck me that it was serious till this morning. Then you betrayed yourself in every word you said. You were madly in love with Maurice.

NURSE (*defiantly*). And if I was, what of it ?

STELLA.   Nothing, except that it's my turn to be shocked. I think it was rather horrible and disgusting. (*She moves away to below the* R. *end of the settee.*)

NURSE (*with increasing emotion*). Yes, I loved him. My love grew as I saw yours fade. I loved him because he was so helpless and so dependent on me. I loved him because he was like a child in my arms. I never showed him my love, I would sooner have died, and I was ashamed because sometimes I thought, notwithstanding everything, he saw it. But if he saw it he understood and was sorry for me. He knew how bitter it is to long for the love of someone who has no love to give you. My love meant nothing to him, he had no room in his heart for any love but the love of you, and you had no use for it. You think you were so kind and considerate. If you'd loved him as I loved him you'd have seen how less than nothing was all you did for him. I could think of a hundred ways to give him happiness, they would have meant nothing to him, and you hadn't the love to think of them.

(*A pause.* STELLA *turns towards the* NURSE.)

STELLA.   Miss Wayland, I'm sorry for what I said just now. It was stupid of me and rather horrid. I suppose there is something beautiful in love, of whatever kind it is. (*Moving a little towards the* NURSE.) Will you let me thank you for the love you gave my husband ?

NURSE (*violently*). No, it's an impertinence to offer me your thanks. (*She moves away, a little up and* L.)

STELLA.   I'm sorry you should think that . . . It's quite true that I didn't love Maurice, at least, not with the love of a woman for a man. I often reproached myself because I couldn't. It seemed so ungrateful and so unkind, but he was no more to me than a very dear friend for whom I was desperately sorry.

NURSE (*looking at* STELLA). Do you think he wanted your pity ?

STELLA.   I know he didn't. But pity was all I had to give him. (*Moving down to below the settee.*) Who was it that said that pity was akin to love ? (*Sitting.*) There's all the world between them.

NURSE (*with angry vehemence*). Yes, all the hideousness of sex.

STELLA.   And do you believe there was nothing of sex in your love for Maurice ?

NURSE (*with a passionate emotion*). No ! No ! My love for that poor boy was as pure and as spiritual as my love for God. There was never a shadow of self in it. I never asked anything but to be allowed to serve and tend him. I never touched his lips till they were cold in death. And now I've lost everything that made life lovely to me. What was he to you ? What was he to his mother ? To me he was my child, my 'friend, my lover, my god. And you killed him.

STELLA (*springing to her feet*). That's a lie !

LICONDA.. Come, Nurse Wayland, you have no right to say that.

NURSE (*beside herself*). It's true and you know it !

LICONDA (*impatiently*). I know nothing of the kind. I only know that you've worked yourself into a state in which you are saying all sorts of things for which you have no justification.

STELLA (*with a tolerant shrug of the shoulder*). My dear, I could no more have killed Maurice than I could walk a tight rope. Doesn't it occur to you that there was nothing to prevent my leaving him ? Who could have blamed me ?

NURSE. How would you have lived ? You haven't a penny of your own. I've heard you tell Maurice a hundred times that you had to mind your p's and q's because he was your only means of livelihood.

STELLA. I certainly shouldn't have repeated a feeble little joke so often. I suppose I could have worked.

NURSE (*scornfully*). You ! Do you know what it means to work for one's living ? All your life you've been petted and spoiled and pampered. And you were going to have a child. How could you have worked ?

COLIN. You're really going too far, Miss Wayland. We can't stand here and let you insult Stella. The situation is preposterous.

STELLA. There was Colin, you know, Miss Wayland. I don't think he would have left me in the lurch.

COLIN. He certainly wouldn't.

NURSE. And what would you have had to go through before he could marry you ? Not only exposure to your husband. But the divorce court. It wouldn't have been a very pretty case.

STELLA. It would have been horrible.

NURSE (*with a gesture towards* COLIN). Do you think his love would have stood that test ? Are you sure he wouldn't have hated you for the disgrace you had thrust upon him ? Men are sensitive, you know, more sensitive than women, and they're afraid of scandal.

STELLA. I may not be typical of my sex. I don't think I should like it either.

NURSE (*with all the scorn of which she is capable*). You don't have to tell me that. Why are you letting me stand here and talk as I'm talking, but that you think you can persuade me or bribe me into holding my tongue ? Why haven't these men, who are your friends and who hate me, thrown me out ? Because they're afraid of me. They're afraid of scandal. They're afraid of publicity. Isn't that true ?

STELLA. Very probably.

NURSE. And you're not only afraid of scandal, you're afraid of your neck.

STELLA. No, that's not true.

NURSE. You were in a hopeless situation. There was only one way out of your difficulties. You know as well as I do that your treachery, your monstrous cruelty would have broken your husband's heart. You couldn't face that. You preferred to kill him.

STELLA (*turning away, to the settee*). You've known me for five years, Nurse Wayland. I don't know how you can think me capable of such wickedness.

(*She sits.* COLIN *sits beside her on the arm of the settee.*)

NURSE. Your husband trusted and loved you. He was bed-ridden. He was defenceless. I know that if you'd had a spark of decent feeling you couldn't have treated him as you did. If you were capable of being unfaithful to him you were capable of killing him.

MRS. TABRET (*with her thin smile*). Are you not falling into a rather vulgar error, my dear ? I know that when people talk of a good woman they mean a chaste one, but isn't that a very narrow view of goodness ? Chastity is a very excellent thing, but it isn't the whole of virtue. There's kindness and courage and consideration for others. I'm not sure if there isn't also humour and common sense.

NURSE (*moving down, R. of her chair*). Are you defending her for having been untrue to your son ?

MRS. TABRET. I'm excusing her, Nurse Wayland. I know she gave Maurice all she could. The rest was not in her power.

NURSE. Oh, I know how you look upon these things. Nothing matters very much. There's no guilt in sin and no merit in virtue. (*She turns away up stage.*)

MRS. TABRET (*rising and moving up* R.C.). May I tell you a little story about myself ? When I was still a young woman, with a husband and two children, I fell madly in love with a young officer who had charge of the police in my husband's district and he fell madly in love with me.

LICONDA. Millie ! (*He sits in the armchair* L.C.)

MRS. TABRET. I'm an old woman now and he's an elderly retired major. But in those days we were all the world to one another. I didn't yield to my love on account of my boys. It nearly broke my heart. Now, you know, I'm very glad I didn't. One recovers from the pain of love. When I look at that funny old-fashioned major now I wonder why he ever excited in me such turbulent emotions. I could have told Colin and Stella that in thirty years it wouldn't matter much if they'd resisted their love. But people don't learn from the experience of others.

NURSE. But you did resist. You can always say that.

MRS. TABRET. I think it was easier then, you know. We attached more importance to chastity than we do now. Yes, I resisted, but

because I know the anguish it was, I feel I have the right to forgive
those who were less virtuous, or perhaps only more courageous,
than I.

(*The* NURSE *moves away to* L.C., *above the table.*)

STELLA. Oh, my dear, you're so kind and so wise.

MRS. TABRET. No darling, I'm only so old.

LICONDA (*rising; kindly, but quite firmly*). Stella, Miss Wayland's
accusation is very definite and must be met.

STELLA. Her accusation is absurd.

LICONDA (*moving to below the chair* R. *of the table*). If Maurice
died of an overdose of chloral, it was administered by somebody.

STELLA. I suppose so.

LICONDA (*moving to the settee*). Can you suggest anyone who
had the slightest motive for wishing he was dead ?

STELLA. No.

LICONDA (*sitting*, L. *of* STELLA). I'm sure you want to help us to
get at the truth. You must forgive me if I ask you some embarrassing
questions.

STELLA. Of course.

(NURSE WAYLAND *moves down* L. *of the table.* MRS. TABRET *sits*
R. *of the table.*)

LICONDA. What did you propose to do when you discovered
you were going to have a baby ?

STELLA. I was frightened. At first I couldn't believe it. I didn't
know what to do.

LICONDA. You were aware that it couldn't be concealed very
long ?

STELLA. Naturally. I thought something would happen. I was
distracted.

LICONDA. Did you tell anyone ?

STELLA. No, I was trying to screw up courage to ask Dr.
Harvester what I had better do. I didn't mind for myself. It was
Maurice I was thinking of.

LICONDA. You must have had some plan.

STELLA. Oh, a hundred. I thought of nothing else day and night.
I tried to find out if there wasn't some place I could go to. I thought
if the worst came to the worst I could get Dr. Harvester to say I
was ill and run down and wanted a change and I could go away till
the baby was born.

LICONDA. I suppose you never thought of making a clean breast
of it to Maurice ?

STELLA. No, never. It would have broken his heart. He would
have forgiven me. He loved me so much. But I couldn't bear that
he should lose his faith in me. It meant everything to him.

LICONDA. You appear to have been the last person who saw him
alive ?

STELLA. Yes, I went in to say good night to him just before I went up to bed.

LICONDA. What did you say to him then ?

STELLA. Nothing particular.

LICONDA. Didn't you say that he'd been very much upset ? He'd cried.

STELLA. Yes. Earlier in the evening, before he went to bed.

LICONDA. Why was he upset ?

STELLA. Need I tell you ? It was so very private.

LICONDA. No, of course not. I have no right to ask you anything. Only there is something very strange about the whole thing and for your own sake I think it would be better if you told us everything.

STELLA. He broke down because he couldn't love me as he wanted to love me. He would have so liked me to have a baby.

LICONDA. And when you said good night to him did he make no further reference to that ?

STELLA. No, none. He'd quite recovered. He was in perfectly good spirits again.

LICONDA. What did he say ?

STELLA. He just asked me if we'd enjoyed our snack and then he said, you'd better get off to bed. I said, I'm simply dropping, and I kissed him and said, Good night, old thing.

LICONDA. How long were you in his room ?

STELLA. Five minutes.

LICONDA. Did he say that he felt sleepy ?

STELLA. No.

LICONDA. I suppose you knew where the chloralin was kept ?

STELLA. Vaguely. I knew that all his bottles and things were in the bathroom. He hated his bedroom to be littered about.

LICONDA. Did he ask you for anything before you went ?

STELLA. No, there was nothing he wanted. Nurse Wayland had fixed him up quite comfortably.

NURSE (to STELLA, *freezingly, moving down* L. *of the table to below it*). You don't understand. Major Liconda is giving you an opportunity of saying that your husband asked you for the chloralin and you, thinking no harm, gave it to him. You saw him take out five or six tabloids and then you replaced the bottle on the shelf.

STELLA (*with irony*). I never thought of that. That would have been quite a good way out if I'd poisoned my husband. (*Turning to* LICONDA.) No, Major, Maurice never asked me for the chloralin and I never gave it to him.

NURSE (*moving below the table to* R.C.). May I ask a question now ?

STELLA. Certainly.

NURSE. Why were you so upset when I came in this morning and told you I'd been into your husband's room ?

STELLA. Do you mean when you said he was dead ?

NURSE. No, you didn't know he was dead then. You couldn't have known unless you'd had second sight.

STELLA. Oh, I see what you mean now. I was angry with you for going into his room before he was called.

NURSE. Are you sure you weren't afraid I'd gone into his room too soon ? Supposing he'd been still alive and it had been possible to save him ?

STELLA. You've quite made up your mind that I murdered Maurice, haven't you ?

NURSE (*turning up* R.C.). I'm not the only one.

STELLA. What makes you think that ?

NURSE (*turning to face* STELLA). Why do you suppose the Major gave you that loophole by suggesting that your husband asked you to give him the tabloids ?

LICONDA (*with some acerbity; rising*). You have done what you thought your duty, Miss Wayland. Well and good. If now you have other things to do, I don't think we need take up any more of your time. (*He turns up, above the settee.*)

NURSE. I'll go. There's nothing more for me to do here. I know you all hate me and you think I've done what I've done from unworthy motives. I started packing my things while you were having lunch. I shall be ready in ten minutes.

MRS. TABRET. You must take your time, Nurse.

NURSE. Believe me, I'm just as anxious to leave this house as you are to get rid of me. I shall be grateful if I can have a taxi rung up.

MRS. TABRET. Colin will get on to the rank. Perhaps you'd better get on at once, darling.

COLIN (*rising and going up* R.). All right, Mother.

(*He opens the door for the* NURSE, *who goes up* R., *and follows her out. The others watch her go in silence. The door is closed.*)

MRS. TABRET. Poor Miss Wayland. She has right on her side, you know, and she feels like a criminal. One can't help feeling sorry for a girl who has so much virtue and so little charm.

LICONDA (*moving slowly across* L.C., *above the table*). Might I speak to Stella alone for a minute ?

MRS. TABRET (*rising*). If you wish to. Come with me, Dr. Harvester.

HARVESTER (*rising*). With pleasure. (*He moves across to* MRS. TABRET.)

MRS. TABRET (*as they move up stage*). It's too bad that you should have to waste so much time on what is no business of yours.

HARVESTER. Believe me, I'd give a farm to be quite certain of that.

(*They go out through the french windows.*)

LICONDA (*moving down* L.C., *after a pause*). Stella, what are you going to do ?

STELLA. I don't know. What can I do ? I feel like a rat in a trap.

LICONDA (*crossing towards the settee*). It's obvious that the matter can't rest here. It can't be hushed up now.

STELLA. What is going to happen, then ?

LICONDA. I suppose Dr. Harvester must communicate with the coroner. There'll be a post-mortem. If, as I'm afraid seems almost certain, Maurice is found to have died of an overdose of chloral there'll be an inquest and we shall have to await the verdict of the jury. (*He turns up* C.)

STELLA. And then ?

LICONDA (*turning to face* STELLA). If they find that poison was administered by a person unknown I imagine that the police will step in. I am afraid you must be prepared for a very terrible ordeal.

STELLA (*rising*). Do you mean that I should be tried for murder ?

LICONDA. It might be that the Director of Public Prosecutions would think that there was insufficient evidence to justify him in instituting proceedings.

STELLA (*moving up to* R. *of* LICONDA). Whatever else I've done you must know that it's incredible that I can be guilty of such a monstrous crime.

LICONDA. Let us get the facts quite straight. I'm afraid it's no good blinking them. You were going to have a child of which Maurice was not the father. You were desperately anxious that he shouldn't know of your condition.

STELLA. Desperately. (*She crosses* LICONDA *to below the chair* R. *of the table, facing down* L.)

LICONDA (*above and on her* R.). Something had happened between you that had greatly distressed him. You were the last person that saw him. He was allowed to sleep on in the morning as long as he could. You were very angry when you found the nurse had gone into his room. He was dead. Five tabloids of chloralin are missing from the bottle and he couldn't possibly have got them himself. Who gave them to him ?

STELLA (*turning to* LICONDA). How can I tell ?

LICONDA (*taking a pace towards her*). My dear, you know that I desire to help you. I am your friend. It's no good beating about the bush. You're in a frightful situation.

STELLA. Do *you* think I'm guilty ?

LICONDA. Do you want the truth ?

STELLA. Yes.

LICONDA. I don't know.

STELLA (*turning away, as though she were thinking it over*). I see. (*She sits.*)

LICONDA (*close to her chair*). Of course, it's only circumstantial, but it all hangs together pretty well. You can hardly be surprised if suspicion falls on you.

STELLA (*with a touch of humour*). It hangs together beautifully. If I didn't know I hadn't poisoned Maurice I should say I must be guilty. There's only one thing I can say on the other side. I should

have thought anyone who knew me at all would know I couldn't
have poisoned Maurice.

LICONDA (*moving away slowly, to the settee*). In the course of my
career I've had to do with a lot of crime. (*Turning to face* L.) To
me one of the shattering things about it has been to notice that the
most law-abiding and decent person may be driven to commit one.
There are very few of us who can say that we shall certainly never
do so. Sometimes crime seems to come to a man as accidentally
as a chimney pot may fall on his head when he's walking down the
street.

STELLA (*with a shudder*). It's rather terrible.

(LICONDA *sits, leaning forward sympathetically.*)

LICONDA (*after a slight pause*). It's not my business to judge you.
I can only feel the deepest sympathy for the dreadful position you
are in. You know what we English are and how uncharitably we
regard sexual deliquencies. A jury would be greatly prejudiced
against you when they were told that you had committed adultery
with your brother-in-law.

STELLA (*looking away*). Poor Colin. He'll have to put up with
a good deal, won't he ?

LICONDA (*looking across at her*). Do you love him very much ?

STELLA. I love him as I never loved Maurice. (*Turning to*
LICONDA.) My love for Maurice was open and sunny. It seemed
as natural as the air I breathe. I thought it would last for ever. But
in my love for Colin there is all my pain and my remorse and the
bitterness of knowing that it's possible for love to die.

LICONDA (*rising*). Yes, that is bitter, isn't it ? (*Turning down* R.,
below the settee.) It makes life look such a sell.

STELLA (*rising*). Wouldn't it be possible in any way to keep
Colin out of it ?

LICONDA (*turning to face her*). Oh, I'm afraid not. Anyhow, that
is a question we can discuss with the lawyers. We must find out
who are the best people to go to. There's one thing I should like
to impress upon you at once. Don't try to hide anything from your
lawyers. The only chance an accused person has is to tell his
advisers the absolute truth.

STELLA (*moving down* L.C.). I have told the truth from the
beginning.

LICONDA. I hope to God you have.

(COLIN *enters up* R., *and moves down.* STELLA *turns and sweeps up
to him,* C., *in a sudden storm of agitation.* LICONDA *turns down*
R. *to the fireplace.*)

STELLA. Oh, Colin, you believe in me, don't you ? You know
I couldn't have done what they accuse me of.

COLIN (*taking her in his arms*). Darling. Darling.

STELLA. Oh, Colin, I'm so frightened.

COLIN. There's nothing to be frightened of. You're innocent.
They can't touch you.

STELLA. Whatever happens it means that we're finished. All
our love is going to be told to everyone and they'll make us appear
beastly and vicious. They'll say horrible things about me. They'll
never know how hard I tried to resist. People blame you because
you fall, they give you no credit for the effort you made to save
yourself. The past counts for nothing.

COLIN. It's so cruel that I who'd give my life for you should
have brought all this misery on you.

STELLA. How can I expect you to stay loving me when we've
gone through what we've got to go through ?

COLIN. I shall love you always. You're all the world to me.
You're all the world I want.

STELLA. Men used to try to flirt with me. It meant so little,
I only laughed at them. Until you came the thought never entered
my head that I could be unfaithful to Maurice. I wasn't troubled.
I just put all that side of life on one side and never thought of it.
I never knew I loved you till it was too late.

COLIN. The only thing I ask you is never to regret that you loved
me, whatever happens.

STELLA. No, I shall never do that. I can't.

COLIN (*with all his tenderness*). Oh, my dear.

STELLA (*desperately, crossing* COLIN *to below the settee*). Major
Liconda, what are we to do ? Can't you say something to help us ?

LICONDA (*very gravely, in a low voice, moving to the* R. *end of the
settee*). How can I advise you ? I can only tell you what I should
do in your place.

STELLA. What is that ?

LICONDA. If I were innocent I should stick it out. I should say
to myself, I may have sinned, I don't know, the world says so and
the world is my judge. Whatever I did, I did because I couldn't
help it and I'm willing to put up with what is coming to me. But
if I were guilty, if in a moment of terror or madness I had committed
an act for which the punishment of the law is death, I wouldn't
wait to let justice take its course. I would take the surest, quickest
way to put myself beyond the reach of the law.

STELLA. I am innocent.

LICONDA. If you hadn't been I should have told you that in
the drawer of my writing-desk is a loaded revolver and that no one
would prevent your going the few steps to my house and letting
yourself in through the study window.

(STELLA *looks at him in horror, fear making her heart beat furiously;
he drops his eyes and turns his head away. There is a terrible
silence.* COLIN *moves to the* L. *end of the settee. Then* NURSE
WAYLAND *comes in and moves down* R.C. *She wears now a coat
and skirt and carries a hat in her hand.* STELLA *pulls herself together.
She addresses the* NURSE *with relief. She is cool and urbane.*)

STELLA (*turning*). You've been very quick, Nurse.

NURSE. I found I had practically nothing left to pack. I've asked Alice to have my trunk taken downstairs.

STELLA. The gardener's here to-day. He can give her a hand.

NURSE. Might I say good-bye to Mrs. Tabret before I go ?

STELLA. I'm sure she'd like you to. She's in the garden.

NURSE. I'll go to her.

STELLA. Oh, don't bother. Colin will call her. (*She sits.*) She only went out because Major Liconda had something he wished to say to me in private.

(NURSE WAYLAND *moves to below the chair* R. *of the table.* COLIN *goes up to the window and calls.*)

COLIN. Mother.

MRS. TABRET (*from the garden*). Yes, darling ?

COLIN. Nurse Wayland is just going. She would like to say good-bye to you. (*He moves down* L.C., *above the table.*)

MRS. TABRET. I'll come.

(*The four persons in the room stand in silence. To all of them the moment is fateful.* MRS. TABRET *comes in, followed by* DR. HARVESTER.)

(*With a little smile as though nothing very serious had happened.*) Is your taxi here, dear ? (*She moves down* R. *of* NURSE WAYLAND.)

NURSE. Yes, I saw it drive up from my window. Mrs. Tabret, I couldn't go without thanking you for all your kindness to me during the three years I've lived here.

MRS. TABRET. My dear, you were never any trouble. It was never difficult to be kind to you.

NURSE. I'm dreadfully sorry to have to repay all you've done for me by bringing this confusion and unhappiness upon you. I know you must hate me. It seems frightful, but I do ask you to believe that I can't help myself.

MRS. TABRET. Before we part, my dear, I should like if I could to release your spirit from the bitterness that is making you so unhappy. God bless you for the kindness you showed my poor Maurice and for the unselfish love you bore him. (*She takes* NURSE WAYLAND'S *hands and kisses her on both cheeks.*)

NURSE (*with a sob*). I'm so desperately unhappy.

MRS. TABRET. Oh, my dear, you mustn't lose your admirable self-control.

LICONDA (*moving in, to below the* R. *end of the settee*). I suppose you will leave an address, Miss Wayland. Dr. Harvester will communicate with the proper authorities and I have no doubt they will want to get into touch with you.

HARVESTER (L. *of the armchair*). I shall go and see the coroner and put the facts before him. Would you like to come with me, Nurse ?

NURSE (*turning to* HARVESTER). No.

HARVESTER. If Mrs. Tabret doesn't mind I'll ring up his place from here and find out if he's in. (*He turns to the desk down* L.)

MRS. TABRET. Of course, I don't mind, but before you do that may I say something ?

HARVESTER (*turning at the desk*). Of course.

MRS. TABRET. I'll try to be brief. (*A moment's pause.*) Nurse Wayland is mistaken in thinking that Stella was the last person who saw Maurice alive. I saw him and spoke to him later.

NURSE (*with utter amazement*). You ! (*She sinks into the chair* R. *of the table.*)

HARVESTER (*moving in, to below the armchair*). But was he wide awake ? If he'd taken thirty grains of chloralin he'd have been certainly very drowsy, if not comatose.

MRS. TABRET. Wait a minute, Dr. Harvester. Let me tell you my story in my own way.

HARVESTER. I beg your pardon. (*He sits in the armchair.*)

MRS. TABRET. You know that Maurice's room was just under mine. His windows were always wide open and when he couldn't sleep, and put on his light, I could see the reflection from my room. Then I used to slip down and sit by him and we'd put out the light and talk about his childhood in India and my own youth. Sometimes we'd talk about things that few men care to speak of in the broad light of day. He'd tell me of his great love for Stella and how anxious he was for her welfare and happiness. And often he would fall asleep and I'd steal softly away. We never mentioned these long conversations we had. I didn't want Stella to think that I was in any way taking her place.

STELLA. My dear, I wouldn't have grudged you anything.

MRS. TABRET (*smiling at* STELLA). There was no need to. (*She pauses and continues.*) I couldn't sleep last night. There was no light in Maurice's room, but I felt strangely that he was lying awake, too. I went downstairs and into the garden and looked in at his window. He saw my shadow and said, " Is that you, mother ? I thought you might come in."

HARVESTER. What time was that ?

MRS. TABRET. I don't know. Perhaps an hour after you'd left. He told me that he'd taken his sleeping-draught but it didn't seem to be having any effect. He said he felt awfully wide awake. And then he said, " Mother, be a sport and give me another, it can't hurt just for once, and I do want to have a decent sleep."

HARVESTER. Somehow or other he was very nervous last night. I suppose his usual dose wasn't any good.

MRS. TABRET (*very quietly*). Very early after his accident I had promised Maurice that if life became intolerable to him I would give him the means of putting an end to it.

STELLA. Oh, God !

MRS. TABRET. I said that if his sufferings were so great that he couldn't bear them any more and he solemnly asked me to help him, I wouldn't shirk the responsibility. And sometimes he'd say to me, " Does the promise still hold ? " And I answered, " Yes, dear, it holds."

STELLA (*with the greatest agitation*). Did he ask you last night ?

MRS. TABRET. No.

LICONDA. What happened then ?

MRS. TABRET. I knew that Stella's love meant everything to Maurice and I knew that she had none to give him because she had given all her love to Colin. What do we any of us live for but our illusions and what can we ask of others but that they should allow us to keep them ? It was an illusion that sustained·poor Maurice in his sufferings, and if he lost it he lost everything. Stella had done as much for him as even I, his mother, could ask of her. I was not so selfish as to demand from her the sacrifice of all that makes a woman's life worth while.

STELLA. Why didn't you give me the chance ?

MRS. TABRET. Years ago, I thought that no greater sacrifice could ever be asked of me. I know now it was nothing. For I loved Maurice. I adored him. I am so lonely now he is dead. It was a lovely dream that he dreamed, and I loved him too much to let him ever wake from it. I gave him life and I took life away from him.

NURSE (*rising, horror-struck*). Mrs. Tabret ! It's impossible ! How dreadful ! (*She buries her face in her hands and moves* L.C., *below the table.*)

(STELLA *sits erect, rigid.* HARVESTER *rises.* COLIN *moves to above and* R. *of the chair* R. *of the table.*)

MRS. TABRET (*a little nearer the settee*). I went into the bathroom and climbed on the chair and got the bottle of chloralin. I took five tabloids, as you know, Nurse Wayland, and I dissolved them in a glass of water. I took it in to Maurice and he drank it at a gulp. But it was bitter ; he mentioned it, and I suppose that's why he left a little at the bottom of the glass. I sat by the side of his bed holding his hand till he fell asleep, and when I withdrew my hand I knew it was a sleep from which he would never awake. He dreamed his dream to the end.

STELLA (*rising and taking* MRS. TABRET *in her arms*). Oh, Mother, Mother. What have you done ? And what will be the end of this ? Oh, I'm so terrified.

MRS. TABRET (*gently releasing herself*). My dear, don't bother about me. What I did I did deliberately and I am quite ready to put up with the consequences.

STELLA. It's my fault. It's my weakness. How can I ever forgive myself ? What have I done ?

(COLIN *moves down a little,* L. *of* MRS. TABRET.)

MRS. TABRET. You mustn't be silly and sentimental. You love Colin and Colin loves you. You mustn't think about me nor distress yourselves at what happens to me. You must go away and then you can marry and have your child and you must forget the past and the dead. For you are young and the young have a right to life and the future belongs to them.

COLIN. Mother, darling. Oh, Mother, you make me so ashamed.

MRS. TABRET. My son, I love you, too. I have your happiness very much at heart. (*She goes to the chair* R. *of the table, and sits.*)

(COLIN *moves to* STELLA.)

LICONDA (*crossing to* MRS. TABRET). Millie. My dear, dear Millie.

MRS. TABRET (*with a slightly grim smile*). Well, Nurse Wayland, you see you were quite right. Of course, I ought to have replaced the tabloids by others, aspirin or chlorate of potash, but as you said just now murderers often make mistakes and I'm not a habitual criminal.

(*There is a moment's pause.*)

NURSE. Dr. Harvester, are you still willing to sign the death certificate ?

HARVESTER. Yes.

NURSE. Then sign it. If there were ever any question I am prepared to swear that I left the tabloids on Maurice's table by his bed.

STELLA. Nurse Wayland !

MRS. TABRET (*to* HARVESTER). Isn't it a dreadful risk you're taking ?

HARVESTER. Damn it, I don't care.

LICONDA. Oh, Nurse, we're so grateful to you, so infinitely grateful.

(NURSE WAYLAND *throws herself down on her knees and clasps* MRS. TABRET *in her arms.*)

NURSE. Oh, Mrs. Tabret, I've been so horrible. I've been petty and revengeful. I never knew how mean I was.

MRS. TABRET. Come, come, my dear, don't let us get emotional. We are both of us lonely women now. Let us help one another. So long as you and I can keep our love for Maurice alive in our hearts he is not entirely dead.

CURTAIN

FURNITURE AND PROPERTY PLOT

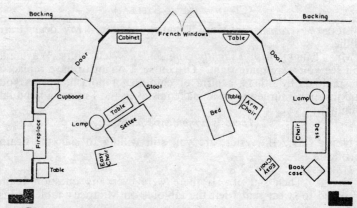

Carpet on stage. Rug at fireplace. Strips in hall and corridor.
Long curtains at french windows.
On walls: Water colours, etchings, photographs.
1 settee (chintz covered).
2 small easy chairs.
1 armchair.
1 stool.
1 small table above settee. (*Act I, whisky, siphon and glasses set.*)
1 round table at L.C.
1 occasional table with flowers, or photograph (*down* R.).
1 writing table (L.) with usual dressing.
1 chair at desk.
1 side table (*up* L.) with photographs and flowers.
1 china cabinet (*up* R.) with tall vase on top.
2 floor standard lamps.
1 corner cupboard.
1 wheeled invalid bed (*Act I*).
On mantel: Large clock, ornaments, photographs, ashtray.

PROPERTIES.
Tapestry work and bag (MRS. TABRET).
Book and needlework (NURSE).
Evening bag and usual contents (STELLA).
Chess board and chessmen.
Off R.: Tray with champagne, ice, and glasses (COLIN).
Silver dish of sandwiches (NURSE).

NOTES ON LIGHTING

ACT I.

The general lighting should be pink and blue, well checked down. Acting areas No. 51 gold, on and around the settee, and from C. to L.C. on and around the table. O.P. standard lamp ON. Amber lengths on interior backings. No. 18 blue floods on exterior.

CUE: *As* COLIN *switches off.* Snap out all lighting, except pool on area L.C. on and around STELLA.

ACTS II and III.

Full, gold and pink. White three-quarters. Lengths as before. Flood on exterior straw and white, full. No CUES.

Any character costumes or wigs needed in the performance of this play can be hired from Charles H Fox Ltd, 25 Shelton Street, London WC2H 9HX.

MADE AND PRINTED IN GREAT BRITAIN BY
WHITSTABLE LITHO LTD., WHITSTABLE, KENT